Engagement

Establishing Relationship in Christ

by

Phillip A. Ross

Pilgrim Platform
Marietta, Ohio

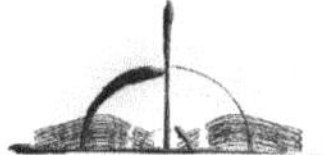

ISBN: 978-0-9820385-2-9

Published by

Pilgrim Platform
149 E. Spring St., Marietta
Ohio, 45750
www.pilgrim-platform.org

Biblical quotations are from the *English Standard Version*, Standard Bible Society, unless otherwise cited.

Printed in the United States of America

To my wife
Stephanie

Table of Contents

Introduction..1
In The Light...5
Of The Last Day...11
God's Revelation..16
Not By Man..28
Laying Down the Law of Grace...33
Show Me...39
Faith's Reward...45
Redemption..50
God The Father...55
God The Son...61
When Nations Stumble...67
The Holy Ghost..71
Regeneration..76
Perseverance..82
Resurrection of Damnation...86
The Resurrection of Salvation..92
Christian Unity...98
Books by Phillip A. Ross..104

Introduction

It is to my embarrassment that this manuscript has sat unpublished for more than ten years. I have edited the material twice but each time I have gotten distracted by other concerns and simply forgotten it. Yet, the most recent edit has been helpful, both to me as I have reviewed this material and to the material because I have been able to see it with more mature eyes this time around. This is only to say that it has been waiting in God's providence for these final touches.

The material here is not my usual fare, but was an attempt to put my best understanding of Scripture and salvation in Christ into a succinct format for a church that did not know me. The first chapter was presented as my candidating sermon, which then became this series following my call and installation, which explains the gap in time between the first chapter (sermon) and the next. It is not an exp0-sitional book study, but is more of a topical study intended to speak to the needs of contemporary people by uncovering various biblical truths and at the same time revealing various contemporary misunder-standings about the Bible and salvation.

After fifteen years of ministry in the United Church of Christ (UCC), I changed denominations and entered the Conservative Congre-gational Christian Conference (CCCC), the only confessional branch of Congregationalism extant at the time. That change brought me to Marietta, Ohio, to serve Putnam Congregational Church, my first CCCC church. This series was preached during my first months there as a way of self-introduction and was aimed at providing grist for church renewal and growth, as the pulpit committee that called me said they wanted.

As you will come to understand, it created quite a stir among those who heard it. But it did not generate church renewal or revival, at least not in the way that anyone would notice, not in what are considered to be the contemporary measures of renewal and revival.

I did not give them what they wanted nor what they expected, but I did my best to give them what God has given me by way of understanding Scripture. What else could I do? This is not to suggest that my understanding is unique, unusual or special in any sense. I don't think it is any of these things, and I pray that it isn't.

Rather, what you will see here is a synopsis of the historic, Protestant, Reformed position. If it seems unusual it is because this theological position has been all but abandoned by the vast majority of contemporary Christians and their churches over the past 20, 50 or 100 years, depending on where you live and what circles you fellowship in. To my surprise, Putnam Congregational Church did not want to be Congregational, at least not in the original, historic meaning of Congregationalism.

I have endeavored to remove references to Congregationalism from the content of these pages and to craft my best understanding of basic Christianity at that time, and have made a few editorial changes in this last editing process. The purpose is to explain Christianity from a biblical and historic perspective, not to convert anyone to the idiosyncrasies of Congregationalism. And yet I cannot be other than who I am, and my Christian upbringing and training have been mostly Congregational.

My prayer is that God's Holy Spirit will provide a generic understanding of God's Word and God's Way as you engage these pages. You will find them challenging, not because of anything I have added, but because God's Word challenges our humanistic understandings at every turn. I pray for your conviction as you engage these pages, that God will break the hard nut of resistance to His Word if He has not yet done so in your life.

Special thanks to my wife, Stephanie, for her love, without which my work would not happen, for proofreading and helping to make this book better, and for her patience and understanding of my need to write.

Phillip A. Ross
September 2008
Marietta, Ohio

In The Light

Nevertheless, many even of the authorities believed in him, but for fear of the Pharisees they did not confess it, so that they would not be put out of the synagogue; for they loved the glory that comes from man more than the glory that comes from God. And Jesus cried out and said, "Whoever believes in me, believes not in me but in him who sent me. And whoever sees me sees him who sent me. I have come into the world as light, so that whoever believes in me may not remain in darkness. If anyone hears my words and does not keep them, I do not judge him; for I did not come to judge the world but to save the world. The one who rejects me and does not receive my words has a judge; the word that I have spoken will judge him on the last day. For I have not spoken on my own authority, but the Father who sent me has himself given me a commandment—what to say and what to speak. And I know that his commandment is eternal life. What I say, therefore, I say as the Father has told me."

—John 12:42-50

These verses provide a summary of Jesus' teaching, much like Moses' farewell discourse (Deuteronomy 30:15-20). It is the very heart of Jesus' teaching. As with all Scripture it is set in a particular context, and the context is instructive.

Jesus had just entered Jerusalem on what we call Palm Sunday. He was teaching sojourners who had come to Jerusalem for Passover. He had predicted His death on the cross, and began talking about who would believe, and who wouldn't. Jesus then began talking about the difference between believers and nonbelievers.

Some from every walk of life believed. Some from every walk didn't. Verse 42 tells us that there were many rulers or upper class people who believed—certainly not a majority, but many. More than a few. However, these upwardly mobile Christians were afraid to confess Jesus, afraid to publicly acknowledge that they believed Him to be the Messiah because such acknowledgment would threaten their social position, "lest they should be put out of the synagogue" (v. 42).

They knew that confession of their belief would not be popular, and that to maintain their ruling positions and their social status they had to appeal to what was popular. Unwilling to cast their salvation upon the Rock of Christ without regard for the prevailing winds of popular religion, they elevated popularity and social position above their commitment to Jesus Christ. Scripture says they loved the praise of men more than the praise of God (v. 43).

Self Reflection

Before we think too critically of them, we must carefully consider our own passion for popularity and position. We must take a close look at ourselves. It is easy to criticize these rulers. Scripture gives us all the ammunition we need. But before we bring them into our sights, we need to point the guns of grace and faith in Christ at ourselves. Before we accuse anyone else of overvaluing the winds of popular opinion, we need to take a critical look at ourselves.

In order to do that we need to know the difference between popular religion and classical (or biblical) Christianity. We must know the earmarks of historic faith, so we can take our cues from Christ. To fail here is to open ourselves to the errors of popular religion.

Everybody likes to think that they know the truth. These rulers that John criticizes thought that they knew the truth. They thought that they could be both popular and faithful. But real Christian faithfulness has never been popular. One of Satan's best ruses is to convince people that Christianity is a popular religion.

These rulers were people who believed in Jesus, but their belief failed to bring them to a confession of faith that was acceptable to God. Faithfulness is God's weapon against the excesses of popularity. It's easy to read that they loved the praise of men more than the praise of God and think that we are not like them. It is another thing to stand for Christ against popular opinion. This is the concern of these verses.

The first thing that Jesus said in response was that His popularity didn't matter because belief in Him constituted belief in God. To believe in Jesus is to believe in God, in Him who sent Jesus. And God is not subject to the whims of popularity.

Of course, the issue of His divinity was the very issue that got Jesus crucified. The Jews accused Him of blasphemy, of claiming to be God incarnate. Indeed, they were right. He did claim that because it was true. Verse 45 is the clearest example of Jesus identifying Himself as God, "he who sees Me sees Him who sent Me." To see Jesus is to see God. Jesus is not the issue here, "seeing" is.

Christians have come to accept Jesus' statement as an ordinary fact of the Bible. But unbelievers today still find this ordinary fact of Christianity to be a major stumbling block. People say, "Sure, Jesus was a great guy, but God! No way." In the face of such unbelief evangelism can easily open the doors of the church to the falsehoods of popular religion by allowing this kind of belief into the church in the name of evangelism.

Church growth gurus today tell us that the hard teachings of Jesus should be avoided because the unchurched won't like them. They counsel preachers to preach only spiritual milk. The church has been fed on spiritual milk for fifty years—the milk of liberalism and socialism. During this period there has been a decided failure of Christian maturity because it is not the gospel, not the Bible that is being taught. This approach, begun in earnest after World War II, brought great popularity to Christian liberalism. The same strategy, dressed up in a new form, now threatens the contemporary Evangelical churches. By contrast Jesus offered this meaty discourse to unbelievers and the barely believing in Jerusalem.

The Light

"I have come as a light into the world, that whoever believes in Me should not abide in darkness" (v. 46). When the light comes darkness is dispelled. But if the coming light is not too near you, and some darkness still abides—even though you see the light in the distance—you are not to continue to abide in the darkness, but move toward the light. In other words, the light of Christ will effect your situation by revealing what abides in darkness. When you see what abides with you in the darkness, you must then move away from it, and come to the light, to Jesus.

The Greek word for church is *ekklesia*, which means a called out people. The church is composed of people who have been called by the Lord out of their sins and out of the sins of society. Paul says that Christians are to be "separated to the gospel of God" (Romans 1:1).

I'm not going to argue for Christian separatism as it is popularly understood. We find too many otherwise faithful Christians thinking that they should create alternative Christian communities or societies that have nothing to do with popular culture. I think that is wrong (and impossible).

But we must also realize that Christians are indeed called to separate themselves from some things and from some people, but not from society as a whole. We are called to be *in* the world, but not *of* the world. We are called to be leaven in the loaf of humanity. We are called to be lamps for the light of Christ. To accomplish these things we must participate in society.

But not in all that society offers. We are to avoid "adultery, fornication, uncleanness, lewdness, idolatry, sorcery, hatred, contentions, jealousies, outbursts of wrath, selfish ambitions, dissensions, heresies, envy, murders, drunkenness, revelries, and the like; of which I tell you beforehand, just as I also told you in time past, that those who practice such things will not inherit the kingdom of God" (Galatians 5:19-21). Whoever believes in Christ should not abide in darkness.

The application here is to discern how to both participate in and be separate from contemporary society. A good place to begin is to evaluate your television watching. If your television exposes you to the list of things to avoid in Galatians 5:19-21, watch something else. Better yet, turn it off. Television is one of the more successful means by which Satan infects most Christians with the evil that God commands us to avoid.

Theology

Verse 47 takes us deeper into the recesses of theology. You know, theology is not really a difficult subject, not for believers. It is Satan who makes theology difficult by muddying the waters. Jesus makes it simple. However, there is one requirement for an effective understanding of theology. One must be a born again believer who relies upon the power and presence of the Holy Spirit. There can be no real understanding of Christ or His gospel without regeneration because God's Word is foolishness to the world (1 Corinthians 1:20). Jesus said, "unless one is born again, he cannot see the kingdom of God" (John 3:3).

The deeper issue in verse 47 has to do with judgment. We know that Jesus is the judge of the world, "For the Father judges no one, but has committed all judgment to the Son" (John 5:22). God has made Jesus the judge of this world. But if that is true, then why does Jesus say here that He will not judge those who don't believe? We know that Jesus will judge both the "good, to the resurrection of life, and those who have done evil, to the resurrection of condemnation" (John 5:29).

The latter surely includes unbelievers.

Here we have the gospel of Christ in its purest form. Yes, Jesus is the judge of the world. But for now he has come to establish His throne of grace, not His throne of judgment. The coming of Christ has provided grace for believers. That window of opportunity is now open to all the world. Believe and be saved. But when Jesus comes again, He will come as judge, and the window of grace will be shut. This is the urgency of the gospel. The window of God's grace will not always be open. People must come to Christ while that window is open because when it is shut there will be no recourse to salvation.

We must also be careful to understand what Jesus meant when He said that He "did not come to judge the world but to save the world." Does He mean to save the whole world? I would like to think that he does because I have a strong emotional attachment to this world and to many of the people in it who are not born again Christians. I would like to believe that Jesus will save the whole world because that would be the humanitarian thing to do.

But that is not what God's Word says. Jesus does not offer universal salvation, He offers particular redemption. Clearly, not everyone has been, nor will be saved. Clearly, not everyone in the world today confesses Christ. And just as clearly, the day of Christ's return is approaching. His return will bring His throne of judgment.

Hell

There is a hell and its jaws yawn wide to devour this perishing world. The jaws of hell are stretching wide today to satisfy Satan's voracious appetite for flesh. In contrast, Jesus commands His followers to "Enter by the narrow gate; for wide is the gate and broad is the way that leads to destruction, and there are many who go in by it" (Matthew 7:13).

Jesus calls His people to offer hope to this world of woe. But the hope we offer must be His hope, not ours. The words of instruction we give must be His words, not ours. The understanding of Scripture that we share must be His understanding, not ours.

Here we find Jesus' own summation of the gospel of grace. The same message that provides hope to the saved frightens everyone else. That is not my particular take on the message. That is Jesus' own summation. It is His Way and His Word. Faithful Christians are simply to study and report it. Let Scripture interpret Scripture, and not mess it up with our futile attempts to make it relevant.

The application of this particular verse is self-analysis. We must examine our own response to the Scripture. If we are assured of our salvation in the face of Jesus' summation of the gospel, then we are to enter into the joy worship, prayer, study, and service. But if we are full of doubts and conflicts, we must enter into worship and make our service the discipline of further study and prayer.

That's basically what the church is: an institution of worship, prayer, study and service. Worship and prayer must inform both our study and our service. And the truth is that no one in this life ever outlives their need for worship, prayer, study, and service.

We didn't complete our examination of these verses this morning. But no matter when we started or when we stopped we would not have finished in a morning. I'm not concerned with finishing this morning. This morning I'm concerned with beginning. I pray we will have another opportunity to worship together.

January 14, 1996

Of The Last Day

When I was here last we did not finish our examination of these verses. I asked the Lord for another opportunity to finish. He has given us that opportunity, so I thought that we should work with what the Lord has given. It's always best to work with what the Lord has given.

The sermon title in January was "In The Light." Today it is "Of The Last Day." Put them together and you have "In The Light Of The Last Day." This is the theme of these verses. Jesus, on His way to Jerusalem for that fateful Passover, provided some final instructions for His disciples. In these few verses we have a summary of the gospel.

Jesus had come in the name and by the authority of God. He does not speak of His own authority. Nor does He merely represent God. He has come on behalf of the Father, but not on behalf of the Father only. His authority is none other than the Triune God—Father, Son, and Holy Spirit. Each Person of the Holy Trinity is distinct, but not separate.

Father, Son, and Holy Spirit do not represent a tri-partisan consensus of opinion, as if they were politicians forging a party platform. Rather, they present the unity of God's truth, manifest in three eternal personalities with whom we can be in personal relationship and communication through God's Word.

To believe on the name of Jesus Christ is to believe on Him who sent Jesus—God the Father. But such belief comes only by the presence and power of the Holy Spirit. To see Jesus as the Son of God, the second Person of the Trinity, is also to see the fullness of God Himself. Why? Because to believe on or see any part of the Trinity requires the presence and power of the Holy Spirit who then mediates both the Father and the Son to the faithful.

All of this is only to say that belief in Christ is a work of God through the Holy Spirit. People cannot work themselves up into an spiritual lather that will produce faith. One of the mysteries of Scripture is that people have the responsibility to believe, but cannot of themselves fulfill that responsibility. The problem prior to Christ was exactly this.

"I'm sorry, you can't get there from here!"

"What then must I do to be saved?"

The answer, then and now, is to pray for God's help. God sent Jesus for this very purpose. Jesus is the only mediator of salvation by faith alone in Christ alone. Salvation is given to everyone who will believe. With the help of the Holy Spirit, people are able to respond to God's offer and receive salvation in Christ and the appropriate gifts of the Spirit.

Light

This is the light that Jesus brought into the world. The ministry of Jesus brought an undeniable light to the ancient doctrine of salvation by faith. Salvation by faith was available in Old Testament days, and is revealed in the Old Testament Scriptures. But its revelation there is spotty and difficult to discern when compared to the clarity of the New Testament.

Faith in Christ cannot go wrong, but people can and do fail to believe in Christ. Here we have a difficulty. Seeing that faith comes by the Spirit, whose fault is it that people don't believe? Belief without the Spirit is impossible, and God dispatches the Spirit to whom He will. So if people don't have the Spirit, is it their fault?

In a word, yes! Here is the mystery. The responsibility for salvation belongs to God, but the responsibility for faithlessness falls to the faithless. If you are saved, God gets all the glory (all the credit), but if you aren't, its your own fault. This is the teaching of Scripture.

Children, if you can understand me right now then you can understand that God commands you to believe. Believing is something you must do. To believe you must read your Bible and pray for God to guide you in all that you do. Ask your parents to help you.

Parents, it is not only your responsibility to believe, but you are responsible to evangelize and disciple your own children. You must teach them to read the Bible and to pray at home, not just at church. You must present the gospel to them. The church's role is to help you, not to do it for you. An hour on Sunday is not enough to counter the lures and lies of Satan.

Grandparents, your responsibility is not only to believe, and not only to teach your children, but to also teach your grandchildren. You have a special opportunity to reteach your own children by teaching your grandchildren in their presence. Let your children hear you and see you teach your grandchildren to read the Bible and to pray.

This mystery of the responsibility of Christian belief is much like the situation regarding the nature of light itself. The scientific theories about light fall into two irreconcilable camps. There is the particle theory and the wave theory. Both theories are internally consistent and both serve to explain much about light. But neither explains everything. So, we ask, is light a particle or a wave? Again, the answer is, yes! Both theories, both descriptions are true and we must hold them together in a kind of creative tension. They are not mutually exclusive, they are just completely different.

Open Gates

Consequently, Jesus can say that He didn't come to judge the world for its faithlessness. He came to receive the glory for its salvation. The purpose of His death on the cross was to open the gates of God's grace to all who believe. His purpose was to be glorified, to receive the glory for the grace of salvation by faith alone. Indeed, the gates of grace are open wide now. Now is the acceptable time of the Lord. Believe now while there is still an opportunity.

When Christ comes again He will come as Judge. His purpose will then be to judge the world, to gather in His harvest, and to close the gates of grace. That day approaches. That day provides the urgency of the gospel. That day is coming down the long, slippery slope to the end of the 20th Century like a history train—fully loaded, fully stoked, and bound for glory.

That day is the concern of the gospel. God's mercy shines on the good and bad alike... until that day. All is well with the righteous and the unrighteous alike... until that day. The nations rage and the people plot their vanities (Psalm 2)...until that day. The saved and the unsaved reap God's mercy...until that day. The regenerate and the unregenerate sit together in church...until that day.

On the last day Jesus will judge both the "good, to the resurrection of life, and those who have done evil, to the resurrection of condemnation" (John 5:29). The point is not that all sinners go to hell. We know that all have sinned and none are righteous (Romans 3:10), and that Christ has come to save sinners. But not all sinners will be saved. We also know that only those covered by the blood of Christ will be saved, which means that the unsaved will find themselves unable to escape eternal punishment in that day.

The last day will be a great and awful day. It will be great for the elect, those who follow through on their responsibility to believe, who yield themselves to the power and presence of the Holy Spirit for guidance and strength.

No Exemptions

But it will be an awful day for those who have heard the offer of the gospel, who sit here today aware of their responsibility, who know of Christ's faithfulness, who know of the strength of the Holy Spirit to accomplish God's purposes, who know that the offer is open to all who believe, but who—for whatever reasons—fail to meet their responsibility to believe on Jesus Christ.

"Take My yoke upon you and learn from Me, for I am gentle and lowly in heart, and you will find rest for your souls" (Matthew 11:29), said Jesus. "This is the will of the Father who sent Me, that of all He has given Me I should lose nothing, but should raise it up at the last day" (John 6:39), said Jesus.

Paul, preaching to the Greeks said, "God...now commands all men everywhere to repent, because He has appointed a day on which He will judge the world in righteousness by the Man whom He has ordained. He has given assurance of this to all by raising Him from the dead" (Acts 17:30-31).

"Therefore, as through one man's offense judgment came to all men, resulting in condemnation"—all are condemned because of Adam's sin, "even so through one Man's righteous act the free gift came to all men, resulting in justification of life" (Romans 5:18). So, all must either receive the condemnation of Adam or justification by faith in Christ. That is the choice. None are exempt. There is no middle ground, no other choice. And the last day is the deadline.

Jesus also said, "I have not spoken on my own authority" (vs. 49). He spoke by the authority of God. I must tell you the same thing. I speak to you today, not on my own authority, but on the authority of Jesus Christ, whom I serve. I am just the delivery boy, God's "gofer." The message is not mine, but Christ's. If you have a problem with the message, take it up with the Lord. Oh, I'll help however I can, but please understand that the message is not mine. My responsibility is simply to deliver it. What you do with it is your responsibility.

Jesus went on, "but the Father who sent Me gave Me a command, what I should say and what I should speak" (vs. 49). After Jesus' resurrection He walked with two disciples on the road to Emmaus. They were going home. They thought Jesus was dead. Sure, there were stories of His resurrection, but even as the Lord walked with them and talked with them, "Him they did not see" (Luke 24:24).

"And beginning at Moses and all the Prophets," Luke tells us, "He expounded to them in all the Scriptures the things concerning Himself" (Luke 24:27). Only when Jesus walked them through a Bible study did they finally see that it was Jesus Himself who instructed them. That's what we will be doing with our time together. We will seek Christ in the Scriptures.

John continues, God's "command is everlasting life" (vs. 50). God has commanded people everywhere to receive everlasting life through faith in Christ. Obeying God's command is itself everlasting life. The door to everlasting life is open today. Tomorrow it may be closed. Won't you enter in? Won't you believe on Christ Jesus today?

April 21, 1996

God's Revelation

For the preaching of the cross is foolishness to those being lost, but to us being saved, it is the power of God. For it is written, "I will destroy the wisdom of the wise, and I will set aside the understanding of the perceiving ones." Where is the wise? Where is the scribe? Where is the lawyer of this world? Has not God made foolish the wisdom of this world? For since, in the wisdom of God, the world by wisdom did not know God, it pleased God by the foolishness of preaching to save those who believe. For the Jews ask for a sign, and the Greeks seek after wisdom; but we preach Christ crucified, to the Jews a stumbling block, and to the Greeks foolishness. But to them, the called-out ones, both Jews and Greeks, Christ is the power of God and the wisdom of God. Because the foolish thing of God is wiser than men, and the weak thing of God is stronger than men. —*1 Corinthians 1:18-25*

In talking with a few people about what I should preach here at Putnam, it was determined that it would be best to begin with the basics. So, I will preach on the classic themes of the Christian faith until the Spirit leads me to do something else.

The beginning point for any discussion of Christianity is the Bible. In order to be on God's team, we must first believe His Word. If we do not believe that the Bible is the Word of God—inerrant, infallible, authoritative, and sufficient, our conversation will fail for lack of common ground. What needs to be said about the fundamentals of the faith cannot be understood without its resting directly upon God's Word.

Because all teaching and doctrine of the Christian faith assume that the Bible is the Word of God, and build upon the foundation of God's Word alone, it is necessary for the sake of discussion to assume that the Scriptures are what they claim to be—even more important for personal faith and salvation itself! If we cannot make this assumption—and it is an assumption grounded in and proven by faith alone, then we cannot begin at all.

Of course, Satan also knows that if he can undermine our trust in the Scriptures at this fundamental level he has won the battle for our souls. His most effective offensive against the Christian faith is to attack God's Word at this fundamental level. The intellectual challenge to the trustworthiness of God's Word by modern liberalism (higher criticism) has been incredibly effective in undermining this fundamental foundation of classic Christianity.

How this has happened is a story of high drama and intrigue. It is a story that has shifted into high gear during the last hundred years. It is my intention to highlight the story without getting lost in the tangle of academic complexity that keeps most of Christendom from even looking into the matter.

First, suffice it to say that God has revealed Himself in nature so that people everywhere believe in the existence of the divine being—excluding atheists, of course. But if you scratch an atheist, an agnostic will bleed. That is to say that there is no such thing as atheism. Atheists are only misguided agnostics—who at least admit their confusion about God, which often hides in great intellectual acumen.

Revelation

Although God is revealed in nature, natural revelation is not sufficient for salvation. Nature only reveals God's existence. Nature reveals the necessity of law and order. Only God's Word provides both law and salvation. God's Word plays a unique role in salvation history, a role that no other religion or philosophy or revelation can play. Scripture is the Rock of salvation. But "If the foundations are destroyed, What can the righteous do?" (Psalm 11:3).

For almost 1500 years the Roman Catholic church preserved the Scriptures. She also preserved them *from* the people. During those years only the aristocracy read, and they only read the Scriptures under the guidance of Rome. The Latin Vulgate (the Latin version of the Bible) was without challenge. Then Erasmus, a Roman Catholic priest suggested some changes in the Latin version based upon his Greek scholarship.

Shortly thereafter Martin Luther was born again as he read

Romans with new insight. Building upon Erasmus' Greek studies Luther translated the Bible into his native German, and Whitcliffe translated it into English. Whitcliffe's translation underwent several minor emendations, but essentially became the King James Version. The King James Version of today is, except for some minor English updates, the King James Version of 1611.

The King James Version is the sole descendant of a family of versions that traces its origin back to the existing Greek manuscripts that are known as the Majority Text. The Majority Text is a Greek translation of the New Testament that is based upon the traditional majority reading of the existing manuscripts.

There are some 5,000 Greek manuscripts in existence today, most of which have been unearthed over the last hundred years, and most manuscripts agree most of the time. But there are variations among them regarding certain passages of Scripture. Most variations are legitimate mistakes made in the process of hand copying, one letter is mistaken for another or one word for another.

Occasionally a copyist-turned-theologian would attempt to improve a passage with his own editorial additions or deletions. Deviant editorial opinion was then disseminated as gospel. The ancient city of Alexandria was notorious for this kind of thing.

Conflict

Add to this situation the conflict brought into the world by Scripture itself. Yes, Scripture—and God Himself—is in conflict with the world. The world is in rebellion against God, against God's Word and God's order. This conflict is as old as Scripture itself. When Satan deceived Eve in the Garden he did it by attacking God's Word.

"Now the Serpent was more cunning than any beast of the field which the lord God had made. And he said to the woman, 'Has God indeed said, "You shall not eat of every tree of the garden"?'" (Genesis 3:1). Satan doubted God's Word. Satan's best shot is always to destroy trust in God's Word. Its much more effective than arguing doctrine.

Satan does not work alone, but has an army of fallen angels and men to aid his cause. From the very beginning of the church the forces of Satan have labored to undermine Christ's salvation work.

We see in Jude that early on Satan began a "fifth column" infiltration of the church in order to corrupt the saints from within. Jude reported that "certain men have crept in unnoticed, who long ago were marked out for this condemnation, ungodly men, who turn the grace of our God into lewdness and deny the only Lord God and our Lord Jesus Christ" (Jude 1:4).

In Jude's day there were leaders in the church, teachers of the gospel who perverted and twisted God's Word into all kinds of nonsense. That effort has continued ever since, corrupting many denominations and their seminaries. Those who continue this effort today are people of great intellectual abilities and tremendous cultural resources. They have been very successful and have multiplied their successes.

My point so far has been to establish the fact that there is a significant theological battle raging about the nature and interpretation of Scripture. The origins of this struggle can be traced back to the dawn of history itself, and will continue until Christ's return. These are the dimensions of the struggle. As I touch upon this issue today you will feel its power. It will make you uneasy, and cause you to question many things you think you know. If you withdraw in fear, your faith will be compromised. But if you trust in the Lord to the end, you will be saved. The issue today focuses on Bible translations.

Veracity

The root of the issue is the trustworthiness of God's Word. If God's Word cannot be trusted completely, Christian faith is seriously compromised. Scripture declares itself to be completely reliable. But if it isn't, we cannot know with certainty which parts are reliable and which are not. Therefore, we cannot trust any of it. It is an all or nothing proposition. We either trust it or we don't.

To set the context, we need to examine the recent history of this conflict. The New Testament was originally written in Greek. Now the first thing to realize is that there are no original Greek manuscripts in existence. All of the 5,000 known manuscripts are copies, the earliest of which are dated to the Second Century. It is important to know this because many contemporary statements of faith declare the reliability of the original Greek manuscripts. "We believe the original Greek manuscripts to be infallible," etc. But we have no originals. No living person has ever seen any originals. So such a statement may not mean much.

What does such a statement of faith say about the actual copies that we have? Can the copies be trusted? Are there any errors in them? Good questions. But with these questions the serpent slithers into our discussion.

Westcott & Hort

In 1881 two English scholars by the names of B.F. Westcott and F.J.A. Hort published a revised Greek New Testament. Previously, scholars had compiled a Greek New Testament for study called the Masoretic Text (or sometimes the Received Text). It is a Protestant venture in that the Roman Catholics continue to rely upon the Latin Vulgate, not the Greek. Nonetheless, the Masoretic Text was the Greek text of the Reformation and stands as the source and foundation of all the classic, Evangelical doctrines of grace.

The Westcott-Hort New Testament was the creation of current (1881) scholarship and archeology. Prior to its publication two Greek manuscripts had been discovered that were believed to be older than any others in existence. They were nearly complete New Testaments. Most of the extant manuscripts contain only selected books, and many are mere fragments. Curiously, one was found in a Catholic monastery, the other in the Vatican Library.

At any rate, these two manuscripts contain significant variations that have generated serious theological differences. There are more than 5,000 differences between the Majority Text and the Westcott-Hort Text, most of which amount to little. But some of the differences affect classic doctrines of the faith, i.e., the divinity of Jesus, the virgin birth, the resurrection, etc. Both of these manuscripts originated in Alexandria, which was a a hotbed of apostasy in the early church.

Nonetheless, Westcott and Hort developed a theory that the oldest manuscripts must be the most accurate. And on that theory they established their 1881 Greek text, favoring the readings of these two manuscripts—which agree with each other only about eighty percent of the time. They forsook the inherited readings of the Majority Text for these two manuscripts, creating a division among scholars, by challenging and changing the established Greek texts to reflect their own modern scholarship.

The long and short of it is that nearly all modern translations since 1881 are based upon the Westcott-Hort Greek Text, rather than the Majority Text of the King James Version. Perhaps you have heard about the King James controversy. This is it. The modern translations follow the Westcott-Hort Text—the Revised Standard Version, the American Standard Version, the NIV, NASV, NKJV, NAS, REB, RSV, CEV, TEV, GNB, Living Bible, Phillips, New Jerusalem, New Century, etc. There have been over a hundred different translations since 1881. Almost every year a new one comes out that promises to speak the current lingo—the latest fashion in God's Word.

The NIV was first published in 1973, revised in 1978 and again in 1984. The Revised Standard Version, first published in 1881, was revised in 1885, 1901, 1946, 1952, and 1971—and gave way to the New Revised Standard Version in 1989. So much for God's never changing Word. All of this is just to say that there are some serious problems in

Bible translation land.

Not So Easy

Children, if you didn't understand everything I said today, that's okay. Just remember this: God's Word is not easy to understand. So, if you have a Bible that is easy to understand, you are probably missing some important parts of God's Word. It's not that the Bible is hard to understand because it is complicated. It's hard to understand because people don't naturally like to hear what it says.

Whatever Bible you read, I highly recommend that you compare it against the KJV. The KJV isn't perfect either, so pray for the Holy Spirit to guide you.

The Bible I use is the New King James Version.[1] It is not without problems either. The reason I use it is because the New Geneva Study Bible comes with the NKJV text, and I trust the people behind the New Geneva Study Bible. R.C. Sproul is the General Editor. One of the reasons I like the New Geneva Study Bible is that it identifies the origin of these textual variances with footnotes. It is the only Bible I know of that does that.

I also trust the New Geneva Study Bible notes. Study notes are a whole other area of concern regarding the personal choice of a Bible. We can talk about that next time.

I still believe the Bible to be the inerrant, infallible, authoritative, and sufficient Word of God. Not just the originals that we don't have, but the copies that we have today—and not just the Greek, but the English as well.

There have always been and will always be interpretive difficulties related to the Bible. The primary key to interpreting the Bible is the presence and power of the Holy Spirit. Without the Holy Spirit no Bible can be understood. But with the Holy Spirit any Bible will prove satisfactory. The concern about versions is a concern of excellence vs. adequacy.

Given these modern interpretative difficulties, many people say that to believe the Bible today is utter foolishness. "Its just a mass of confusion," they say. And the confusion gets piled higher and deeper every year. But in spite of the difficulties, "the message of the cross is foolishness to those who are perishing, but to us who are being saved it is the power of God" (1 Corinthians 1:18).

April 28, 1996

---

1 Since writing this (1996) I have used the Modern King James Bible and currently use the English Standard Version.

The Roar of the Crowd

To whom shall I speak and give warning, That they may hear? Indeed their ear is uncircumcised, And they cannot give heed. Behold, the word of the Lord is a reproach to them; They have no delight in it. Therefore I am full of the fury of the Lord. I am weary of holding it in. "I will pour it out on the children outside, And on the assembly of young men together; For even the husband shall be taken with the wife, The aged with him who is full of days. And their houses shall be turned over to others, Fields and wives together; For I will stretch out My hand Against the inhabitants of the land," says the Lord. "Because from the least of them even to the greatest of them, Everyone is given to covetousness; And from the prophet even to the priest, Everyone deals falsely. They have also healed the hurt of My people slightly, Saying, 'Peace, peace!' When there is no peace. Were they ashamed when they had committed abomination? No! They were not at all ashamed; Nor did they know how to blush. Therefore they shall fall among those who fall; At the time I punish them, They shall be cast down," says the Lord. —*Jeremiah 6:10-15*

Last week we talked about the variety of Bible translations that have flooded the market over the past hundred years. We saw that the publication of the Westcott-Hort Greek Text in 1881 was the source of these variant translations. The King James Version alone comes from the traditional Greek text (the Masoretic Text) of the Protestant Reformation.

However, the astute Bible student will notice that his NIV does not indicate that it is a translation of the Westcott-Hort Greek Text, but of the Nestle-Aland Greek Text. What gives?

In order to make a point I didn't finish the story. The story of the modern Bible translations is much more convoluted than I have indicated. The Westcott-Hort text created such a stir that it became unacceptable to the common people of the church. Consequently, other scholars got involved and massaged the manuscripts again, using essentially the Westcott-Hort textual theories, and the so-called higher criticism. This resulted in the development of yet another Greek text, the Nestle-Aland Text. But because the Nestle-Aland Text was built upon the liberal theories of textual criticism it is the child of the Westcott-Hort, higher criticism, liberal establishment.

While the liberal theologians work to convince the church that there is no tenable alternative, there is a long line of highly competent scholars who defend the Masoretic Text. The so-called "fundamentalist controversy" of the 1920s was about this very issue—the reliability of the traditional text and theology of the Protestant Reformation. The reliability of the Bible is always the issue that takes a thousand forms in its attack against God and His people.

But enough about translations for now. I just want you to be aware that there is a serious controversy raging about the correct translation of the Bible and orthodox belief.

Bible Study Notes

There is a related concern that is just as convoluted—Bible study notes. We are talking about footnotes that help explain what the Bible means. If you have been to a Christian bookstore recently you know that there are a variety of Bibles. There are Bibles of every imaginable stripe. There are different versions—we've covered some of that, and there are different study notes that are integrated into the various versions.

Probably the most famous study Bible of all time—and the first—is the Scofield Reference Bible. C.I. Scofield, a Confederate soldier, was converted in St. Louis. He pastored a Congregational church in Dallas, Texas, and took over Moody's church in East Northfield, Massachusetts, in 1895. He went on to become a traveling evangelist and published his famous Scofield Reference Bible in 1909.

The Scofield Bible is the King James Version with systematic footnotes that promote his dispensational, premillenial theology, a deviation from the traditional Protestant Reformed theology. His theology was—and is—the preeminent expression of what we call fundamentalism.

It is not difficult to see that popular theology, which grew considerably with Scofield, has buried classic theology in a flood of versions and study notes that question the traditional perspective. Go to any Christian bookstore and you will be inundated with a proliferation of Bibles—all claiming to teach the truth, yet all professing central theological differences.

There you will find the International Inductive Study Bible, the Rainbow Study Bible, Catholic Study Bible, Experiencing God Study Bible, Thompson Chain Study Bible, Spirit Filled Life Bible, Open Bible, Full Life Study Bible, Defender's Study Bible, Inspirational Study Bible, the New Scofield Study Bible, the Ryrie Study Bible, Disciple's Study Bible, Student Bible, Quest Study Bible, Oxford Annotated Bible, Harper-Collins Study Bible, Passages of Life Study Bible, Dake's Annotated Reference Bible, Serenity New Testament, Serendipity Bible, Children's Ministry Resource Bible, Comparative Study Bible, Life Application Study Bible, Women's Devotional Bible, to name a few. Most of these are available in the NIV, NASB, NRSV, KJV, NKJV, hard cover, soft cover, leatherflex, slimline, pocket edition, large print, blue, burgundy, black, etc. The list goes on and on.

This is not all bad. Don't get me wrong, Bible study is good. Just realize that all study Bibles—like all churches and all preachers—do not teach the same biblical perspective. In fact, the Bible is the most controversial book ever written. The truth of the matter is that the church today is more confused than ever because it listens to so many opposing voices and attempts to believe them all, or at least most of them. The advent of radio and modern print media have brought the cacophony of theological voices into every Christian home and church, in the city, in the country and in the burbs.

Deviation

The primary point of this exercise is to indicate the many deviations from the traditional Protestant Reformed theology that produced the American nation and the most effective evangelistic effort the world has ever seen. And to suggest that since the high point of the foundation of America and the Great Awakening, the theological course of Western Christianity has been toward confusion and ineffectiveness. Our churches grow weaker with every passing generation.

The point is to notice that the variant theological voices of the last hundred years have all but eclipsed traditional Protestant Reformed theology. The popularity of dispensationalism and premillenialism have overshadowed the foundational teachings of the Protestant Reformation. During the same period, the church has generally gone to seed—declined in faithfulness and strength.

Methodist churches no longer adhere to traditional Methodist theology, not all Presbyterians are Presbyterian, not all Catholics are Catholic, nor Baptists Baptist, etc. The people in pulpits and pews drink from every conceivable theological stream—Christian and nonchristian, and don't realize the irreconcilability of the perspectives from which they dip.

Nonetheless, people grow a little in their faith, going along with what they currently hear or read. But they don't realize that they are caught up in the shifting winds of theological popularity—winds that are themselves driven by the almighty dollar. Christian media is today driven by secular business values. It is a profit venture and deceives the government about its non-profit status. Church today is big business.

Leadershit

There is an additional difficulty that causes dissension in contemporary churches—leadership. It is the pastor's job to sort out and lead the way through this theological maze of confusion and contradiction. Faithful pastors work hard to make sense of all this. But when they teach a particular theological perspective from the pulpit, they are bound to cross swords with some other theological perspective that exists in the pews—only because every possible perspective is represented in the pews of every church of whatever denomination or no denomination.

When this happens some people choose to trust themselves or their favorite Christian media personality over their pastor. Rather than study and discuss the matter with their pastor, people gossip and backbite. Churches today are full of this because society generally is full of it. And the churches are just like the society, to their shame.

What is worse is that the theological nature of the conflict is often misconstrued as personality conflict. It is more acceptable to think of human differences in terms of personality conflict than theological conflict. When differences are a matter of personality, no one is right, nor anyone wrong. But if the differences are theological, some may be more right than others. And repentance is difficult for the stiff-necked and impossible for the proud.

The liberals have an easier go of it. The liberal perspective insists that all theological opinions are equally valid, that all perspectives are relative. Liberalism teaches that there is no orthodox, correct biblical understanding. In doing so liberalism has cut out the very heart of the gospel by redefining it according to personal preference. But it has found a way to end the bickering. Nothing ultimately matters, so there is no reason to fight about anything—unless you disagree with them. Disagree with the relativity doctrine and you will find yourself under serious attack.

Conflict

The result of all of this has been the decimation of traditional faithfulness among churches and Christians of every stripe. The bottom line has been the confusion of the gospel, and the ineffectiveness of the church. The church falters in disarray, locked in self-inflicted conflict, and the watching world walks away in disbelief.

Pastors and people are increasingly lost in the bickering flood of conflicting claims. Meanwhile the world tumbles toward the ever widening gates of Hell. And Satan laughs in delight. The same situation existed during the ministry of Jeremiah. You would think that somewhere along the line God's people would learn.

Jeremiah stands as a case in point. Look again at Jeremiah 6:10-15. Jeremiah wanted to warn his people of their impending danger, but no one could hear him because no one was listening. People no longer paid attention to their pastors or prophets. Because God had been gracious and merciful in the past, they thought that God would always be gracious and merciful—no matter what. They were wrong.

Jeremiah struggled to correct this common misunderstanding about God. But there was no one who could hear him because the people were content with the hirelings who tickled their ears with words of diversity—love, peace, relativity, and the pursuit of happiness.

The most damning accusation that Jeremiah made—which can be made again today—was that people did not know how to blush. Nothing, no matter how vile or sinful, surprised or embarrassed them. They took it all in stride. When the public exposure of sin no longer embarrasses or shames people, the church has lost her moral power. As spiritual discipline fades, spiritual corruption increases.

If you find yourself asking what made Jeremiah think that he was any different from the rest of the religious crowd, you have already slid down the slippery slope of liberalism—doubting God's Word. God made Jeremiah different. Jeremiah was Spirit-led, and his record in Scripture witnesses to the truth he taught. To question Jeremiah's authority is to doubt God's Word.

Hope

Our only hope today is to return to God's Word—to trust it, to study it, to learn it. I invite you to stake your claim on God's Word. To return to the theology of the Protestant Reformation with new eyes, not try to return to the Seventeenth Century, but to see biblical Christianity afresh. The Protestant Reformation was itself the recovery of the gospel that had been obscured by the sinfulness of the churches. Every great movement of the Spirit begins with a return to God's Word and the ancient doctrines of grace. Everything else is apostasy.

Let us together stake our claim on God's Word, and by the presence and power of the Holy Spirit upon the classic doctrines of salvation by faith alone through grace alone in Christ alone to all who will believe. Turn to Christ and be saved from this perishing world. If you have never made public profession of Christ, then I urge you to do so before it is too late.

But don't think that the public nature of confession makes it real. It is real enough for God in the privacy of your own thoughts. We do it publicly only as an expression of thankfulness and obedience. Public confession is not a work of righteousness, but an assenting expression of gratitude.

Pray right now in your own words, right where you sit. Then let's talk about thankfulness, obedience, and our witness to the watching world.

May 4, 1996

Not By Man

For we did not follow cunningly devised fables when we made known to you the power and coming of our Lord Jesus Christ, but were eyewitnesses of His majesty. For He received from God the Father honor and glory when such a voice came to Him from the Excellent Glory: "This is My beloved Son, in whom I am well pleased." And we heard this voice which came from heaven when we were with Him on the holy mountain. And so we have the prophetic word confirmed, which you do well to heed as a light that shines in a dark place, until the day dawns and the morning star rises in your hearts; knowing this first, that no prophecy of Scripture is of any private interpretation, for prophecy never came by the will of man, but holy men of God spoke as they were moved by the Holy Spirit.

—2 Peter 1:16-21

As we move from the discussion of versions and footnotes we must at the outset acknowledge that the authority of the Bible depends upon God, not upon man. At the point that the authority of the Bible is undermined or doubted, spiritual growth is frozen. If we do not trust the Bible, we cannot trust God. And not trusting God we will not enter into a saving relationship with Him.

Casting doubt on God's Word is Satan's most effective means of destroying the reality of salvation. Without trust in God's Word people do not seek God nor progress in spiritual knowledge. Now, it must be reiterated that we are not saved by our knowledge of the Gospel. Rather, salvation is presented by means of God's Word. It is the blood of Christ that saves by faith alone in Christ alone. Faith in Christ is mediated by God's words. God uses His Word as the primary means of salvation. The faith that is necessary for salvation is primarily faith in the trustworthiness of Jesus Christ, who is accurately and honestly revealed through God's Word.

Men were obviously involved in the writing of the Bible. However, God's Word comes not from the minds of men but from the mind of God. Isaiah 55:9 tells us that the heavens are higher than the earth, and God's ways are higher than our ways, and God's thoughts higher than human thoughts.

Trustworthy

Let us, then, trust God's Word to be what it claims to be. From the very beginning we must make this assumption. If we fail to make this assumption, we will not understand one another, nor will you understand or benefit from Scripture. Faith in God's Word (trust in its reliability) is absolutely essential to salvation and for gospel understanding.

When people assume that God's Word is what it claims to be—not just think that it is true but actually believe it with all their heart, mind, spirit, and soul—then God's Holy Spirit can reach into the human soul and touch His people because of the connection made through this common assumption. Psalm 42:7 describes it as deep calling unto deep. More than simply call, God's Word connects with God's Spirit deep in the human soul. This connection is necessary for an effective understanding of God's Word. Without it there is only misunderstanding and confusion because thinking is not grounded on the assumption of God's veracity.

If we do not trust this process, or doubt the reality of God or His Word, or His ability to make this connection and to make it real, then we will not allow ourselves to be available to God. We will turn away from God in disbelief. When this connection is made it is all God's doing. When it is not, it is entirely our own human doing that denies it.

It is in this way that the divine authority of Scripture "is from the inward work of the Holy Spirit bearing witness by and with the Word in our hearts" (Westminster Confession of Faith, 1:5). In other words, there are two witnesses to the truthfulness of God's Word. First, God witnesses to His own veracity, and His witness is sufficient. But in His grace and mercy He allows another witness.

The second witness is the heart of the faithful believer. When a person trusts God and His Word, the Holy Spirit forges a spiritual connection between the believer and God's Word. That connection then provides an undeniable proof of the validity of God's Word—undeniable because it is the believer's own witness. The person who trusts God and His Word becomes his own witness to the trustworthiness of God.

John 16:13-14 tells us of the reality of this process, "when He, the Spirit of truth, has come, He will guide you into all truth; for He will not speak on His own authority, but whatever He hears He will speak; and He will tell you things to come." All Christians are, therefore, Spirit-led. If the Spirit does not lead you, you are not truly Christian. There is no such thing as a Christian who is not Spirit-led. If the Spirit does not lead you, then the Spirit of Christ is not in you, and you cannot actually be a Christian.

Application

There are two applications of this insight. First, Christians cannot rely upon themselves or upon other people—not upon those who claim to be Christian, nor upon those who have university or academic credentials. Not even a seminary degree can provide the trust that is accorded through the gospel. In fact, degrees fall under the condemnation of "tradition of men" (Mark 7:8) when they are elevated to the role of theological determination.

Universities cannot make Christians. Academics cannot make Christians. Nor do seminaries make Christians. Only God by the presence and power of the Holy Spirit can make a Christian. It requires God's hand to provide faith in the heart, confession in the mouth, repentance of the lifestyle, and conversion of the mind. A Christian is not just a changed person. He is a new person, a new creation. And that requires God's creative power.

The second application is that there must be great caution regarding this issue of being Spirit-led. Being Spirit-led does not mean something is true just because a Christian thinks it's true. It does not mean that every thought a Christian has is a revelation from God. To believe our own thoughts is to trust in ourselves. That is not what being Spirit-led means. Christians don't determine the marks of a Spirit-led life, God does.

The concern here is discerning the Word of God. Faithful Christians must trust and believe the Scriptures—yet cannot go beyond the Scriptures. We live in an age of philosophical speculation about all kinds of things. Speculation is the Spirit of the Age today. Much of what we believe to be true is nothing more than imaginative speculation. Faithful Christians are not to be led by the Spirit of the Age, but by the Holy Spirit of God as revealed through the Bible.

We are to follow Scripture. Therefore, we cannot go where Scripture does not go. We cannot say what Scripture does not say. We cannot speculate about the nature of reality, or the nature of man, or the nature of God beyond what is revealed in the Scriptures. What we think we know beyond Scripture is mere speculation, and has no place in faithfulness. "Nothing is to be added (to Scripture), whether by new revelations of the Spirit, or traditions of men" (Westminster Confession 1:6).

This is a most difficult issue for people today and for the contemporary church. I know because I have repented of this habit of speculative thinking. Intellectual speculation is the method of modern academics taught in our schools. We are taught to speculate from a very early age. We are taught that this kind of thinking is the essence of intelligence itself—which is true. But it is the essence of human intelligence, and is the ground of worldly wisdom.[2]

Paul wrote in 1 Corinthians 1:21, "Has not God made foolish the wisdom of this world?" Paul spoke "wisdom among those who are mature, yet not the wisdom of this age, nor of the rulers of this age, who are coming to nothing" (1 Corinthians 2:6).

God is not the philosophical ground of the wisdom of the world, nor does His Word augment or supplement the wisdom of the world—it confounds it. The wisdom of the world—university and seminary academics—do not lead to, nor do they reveal the wisdom of God.

Rather, God is opposed to the wisdom of this perishing world. God's Word runs counter to the wisdom of the world. God's Word turns the wisdom of the world upside-down and inside-out. God's Word cuts across the grain of the assumptions of this world. God's Word rubs the fur of the worldly cat the wrong direction, and the cat doesn't like it!

It's not that God is opposed to academic or intellectual thinking. It is just that the intellect must serve God. God does not play second fiddle to human intelligence. The human mind is a great asset when it serves the Lord, and a great detriment when it does not.

God stands in opposition to the world. God wants to upset our comfortable, worldly assumptions because as long as we cling to the wisdom and assumptions of this perishing world, we cannot cling to the wisdom and assumptions given by God. It is not a both/and proposition. It is an either/or proposition. We cannot love both God and the world. Rather, we can only love either God or the world (Matthew 6:24).

The difficulty is that modern people are schooled to be both/and

2 For more on the confusion of gospel wisdom with worldly wisdom see *Arsy Varsy—Reclaiming The Gospel*, by Phillip A. Ross, Pilgrim Platform, Marietta, Ohio, 2008.

people, and to consider either/or people to be narrow minded. Everything in modern society attempts to teach us that we can embrace both God and the world. But when we do, we only confuse ourselves and contaminate God's purity. From the perspective of the world, faithfulness means spiritual narrow-mindedness.

A television interviewer was interviewing a Baptist pastor. Baptists are known by the world for their narrow-mindedness. The interviewer asked incredulously, "Are you really so narrow-minded as to believe that only Baptists will go to heaven?" The preacher thought a moment and replied, "No," he said, "I'm so narrow-minded that I don't even believe that all Baptists will go to heaven."

Spiritual narrow-mindedness is not a defect, but is the spiritual reality of faithfulness itself. Jesus said,"Enter by the narrow gate; for wide is the gate and broad is the way that leads to destruction, and there are many who go in by it" (Matthew 7:13).

It is God who calls. It is God who saves. It is not by man, nor by the wisdom of man. Salvation is by the initiative and wisdom of God, by grace alone through faith alone in Christ alone.

May 12, 1996

Laying Down the Law of Grace

"Do not think that I came to destroy the Law or the Prophets. I did not come to destroy but to fulfill. For assuredly, I say to you, till heaven and earth pass away, one jot or one tittle will by no means pass from the law till all is fulfilled. Whoever therefore breaks one of the least of these commandments, and teaches men so, shall be called least in the kingdom of heaven; but whoever does and teaches them, he shall be called great in the kingdom of heaven. For I say to you, that unless your righteousness exceeds the righteousness of the scribes and Pharisees, you will by no means enter the kingdom of heaven.

—Matthew 5:17-20

God began, not with law, but with grace. God created the world, not because He had to, not because it was the fulfillment of the laws of nature, but because He wanted to. God created a beautiful world because He loves beauty. The creation of man, like the creation of the world, was never a function of the law, but always of grace.

Abraham was chosen to be the seed of salvation—not because of anything he had done, but simply because of God's will and grace. Abraham was given marching orders to leave Ur and head for the promised land. And he went, not knowing his final destination, but trusting in God. God accounted Abraham's trust (or faith) as righteousness. God knew that righteousness begins with faith in Christ and matures over time. Abraham trusted Christ prior to His incarnation in Jesus of Nazareth. God also knew His own ability to insure that Abraham's faith would produce righteousness—and not just for Abraham, but eventually through Jesus Christ, for all who believe.

Abraham was accounted righteous by his faith in God's Messiah before Moses laid down the law. Righteousness and its salvation have never come because of the law, but always because of God's grace. The law alone cannot produce righteousness, nor does righteousness alone produce salvation. Righteousness is a gift of the Holy Spirit. Where righteousness exists it is wrought by the presence and power of the Holy Spirit, not by the strength or excellence of men. Salvation is a product of the Holy Spirit in the lives of people.

Men cannot attain to righteousness without the presence and power of the Holy Spirit because men are fallen into sin. And the sin we have fallen into is not of our own making—although people continue to make it worse. Sin did not come by human action in the first place. It was a response to Satan's lies. Therefore, people cannot extract themselves from it by means of human action. People cannot stop themselves from believing Satan's lies. Apart from God, people only know Satan's lies.

The Pit

The sin we suffer is at root a pit dug by Satan and fallen into by Adam. Adam's children continue to live in the pit because they cannot get themselves out of it. People can only be extricated from the pit with help from outside the pit. It is too deep. The walls are too high. People are unable to escape from it without help.

Add to this tragedy the fact that people are too proud to accept help, and you have a situation that is not only beyond the ability of man but beyond the will or desire of man as well.

The pit of sin is so big that it does afford a certain living space. And after a while the unscalable walls of the pit are accepted as unalterable—normal—and, consequently, ignored. Over time the reality of sin becomes so accepted as to be disregarded, and even denied by those who dwell in its depths. They know nothing other than life in the pit and disparage any hope of ever escaping the pit as imaginary.

The only escape possible is extrication by God. Salvation is a matter of God's will and God's strength, not ours. Yet, because of God's loving nature and great mercy He will not force His advice or His solution to the problem of sin upon those He loves. God will not force people into salvation. People cannot be saved unless they actually want to be saved, and they cannot want to be saved unless they understand their need for salvation, and they cannot understand their need for salvation apart from the power and presence of the Holy Spirit in their lives, who provides a voice and view from outside the pit. For the most part, as long as the status quo is not threatened, people will see no need of salvation.

Schoolmaster

Consequently, even though salvation comes by grace, it is the function of God's Law to demonstrate to people their personal need for salvation, and their inability to get it without God's help. The law functions as God's schoolmaster. The schoolmaster can gather the students and teach them, but he cannot make them learn.

The role of the schoolmaster is objective, it is imposed from without. Those who would learn must be gathered and taught, for without gathering and teaching there can be no learning. Yet, learning is subjective and requires the desire to learn.

School teachers today are discovering that they cannot force children to learn. Teachers can teach until they are blue in the face, but without the student's desire to learn, teaching is in vain. Yet, if teaching is abandoned, even those who desire to learn will not learn. The solution is not to abandon teaching, nor to try to force children to learn.

There are two biblical approaches to this situation. The first approach is to inspire children to want to learn. Inspiration—desire—is the high road. It is full of hope and zeal. The second road, lower but equally effective, is to frighten people with the stark reality of their personal need and inability, to introduce them to the fear of the Lord. Both are biblical. Both are effective. Both are necessary.

By itself, the mere desire to learn—without discipline and the work of teaching—is ineffective. Education requires more than desire, and more than opportunity. It requires both desire and opportunity, of course. But desire alone (without opportunity) cannot learn, and opportunity alone (without desire) will not learn.

Applying this to salvation, God's law provides the opportunity and the Holy Spirit provides the desire. The law lectures and disciplines. The law supplies intellectual content and experiential consequence. Obedience brings knowledge, disobedience brings consequence. The Bible supplies the objective content (the law), the Holy Spirit supplies the subjective willingness to attend to the content. Both are necessary, neither are sufficient in themselves.

Chicken/Egg

Trying to determine which comes first is like the chicken and the egg conundrum. The human intellect by itself cannot determine which came first. The reality of history is that we are so far beyond the original creation of the chicken/egg that such knowledge is not available to us. We have chickens and we have eggs. Eggs produce chickens, and chickens produce eggs. From a certain perspective it doesn't matter which came first. All we know is that they work together.

But God knows which came first, and Scripture reveals it. The chicken came first because God created a full blown, fully functional world. "God said, 'Let the earth bring forth grass, the herb that yields seed, and the fruit tree that yields fruit according to its kind, whose seed is in itself, on the earth'; and it was so." (Genesis 1:11). The egg is a kind of chicken seed.

We don't want to get too carried away with this sort of analogy. But we do want to point out that Scripture reveals that man cannot know the truth by means of his own experience. Scripture also reveals the correct order of nature, not just the natural order, but the created order.

The correct application of this insight is critical. Again, the insight is that God's Word provides general rules or principles for individuals and societies—not just Christian societies, but all societies and, therefore, all people. The failure to apply God's principles is not only against Christian prudence, but against nature itself. God's principles set things (including men and societies) in their correct order, where "correct order" yields sustainable development.

Right application here is twofold because salvation requires both law and grace—and the order is significant! The fruit of God's principles is salvation, and salvation requires the correct ordering of its constituent parts. Getting it right means understanding whether law precedes grace, or grace precedes law.

In presenting the gospel of salvation are we to present God's grace before we present God's law, or law before grace? It is not that the correct order of presentation will save people. No one will be saved by a correct presentation of the gospel. People are saved by grace alone through faith alone in Christ alone. However, it may well be that an incorrect order of presentation may hinder salvation because, whereas salvation is God's doing, the lack of salvation is human doing (see Deuteronomy 30:19, Luke 10:42, and John 15:16).

Another way to say the same thing is that faithful Christians are called to obedience, and obedience to Scripture requires following God's revealed order. Everything we do must be done according to Scripture, particularly the things related to salvation.

Law/Grace

I want to suggest that the dual nature of salvation—law and grace

—requires a similar duality regarding the presentation of God's promises as revealed in Scripture. God began with individuals—Noah, Abraham, Isaac, Jacob, etc. God chose them and saved them by grace alone. God preserved Noah, and promised Abraham that he would be the father of many nations. Only as Abraham's children grew into nationhood, did God give Moses the law.

The law is divided into two tablets. One reveals the proper personal relationship with God, the other reveals proper social relationships between people. The law itself has a dual nature, prescribing correct personal relationship with God, and correct social relationships according to God's created order.

When dealing with individuals, God applies grace. But when dealing with societies, God applies law. Why this order? The law reveals the personal need for grace, which is the only possible solution to the demands of the law. But notice that both grace and law are supplied by God. Whether a person is in need of grace to answer the demands of the law, or in need of the law to reveal his need of grace, the bottom line is human dependence upon God for salvation.

The point is that grace and law work together, or they don't work at all. Where the law is lacking, the law needs to be applied. Where grace is lacking, grace needs to be applied. But where there is an over abundance of concern for the law, an emphasis on grace will balance matters. And where concern is too narrowly focused on grace, the law needs additional emphasis.

Today, the historic, Protestant, Reformed perspective—the heart of American Christianity—needs fixing at both ends of the theological spectrum. The liberals overly rely on grace, thinking that salvation is universal, that nothing is required of man. The liberals need to hear the law again, for the law specifies God's righteous requirements.

On the other hand, the legalists (fundamentalists) overly rely upon the law, thinking that obedience to the law will save them. They believe that obedience of the law is humanly possible, and strive to accomplish it. The legalists needs to hear the doctrines of God's grace again.

The call of faithful Christians—and historic, Protestant, Reformed churches—is to hold the central ground of orthodoxy against the liberals on the one hand and the legalists on the other. Of course the greatest threat to those in the middle is the temptation to just sit on the theological fence, to take no position at all, to be neither hot nor cold. But such a position is disastrous and will correctly be rejected by all parties, including God (Revelation 3:16).

The fine line of faithfulness requires spiritual grounding to keep from falling to the left or the right. But it does not mean simply sitting on the fence, doing nothing, going nowhere. It does not mean no movement at all! Faithfulness always moves forward—Godward, not swerving to the right nor to the left, but keeping straight ahead, maintaining balance by relying upon the center of gravity itself—Jesus Christ.

We cannot ignore the law. We must live it, teach it, preach it, and evangelize with it. Nor can we forget God's grace. We must also live, teach, preach, and evangelize with grace. We cannot sit like spiritual bumps on God's log, but must move forward in faithfulness.

May 19, 1996

Show Me

Then Moses said to the Lord, "See, You say to me, 'Bring up this people.' But You have not let me know whom You will send with me. Yet You have said, 'I know you by name, and you have also found grace in My sight.' Now therefore, I pray, if I have found grace in Your sight, show me now Your way, that I may know You and that I may find grace in Your sight. And consider that this nation is Your people." And He said, "My Presence will go with you, and I will give you rest." Then he said to Him, "If Your Presence does not go with us, do not bring us up from here. For how then will it be known that Your people and I have found grace in Your sight, except You go with us? So we shall be separate, Your people and I, from all the people who are upon the face of the earth." So the Lord said to Moses, "I will also do this thing that you have spoken; for you have found grace in My sight, and I know you by name." And he said, "Please, show me Your glory." Then He said, "I will make all My goodness pass before you, and I will proclaim the name of the Lord before you. I will be gracious to whom I will be gracious, and I will have compassion on whom I will have compassion."But He said, "You cannot see My face; for no man shall see Me, and live." And the Lord said, "Here is a place by Me, and you shall stand on the rock. So it shall be, while My glory passes by, that I will put you in the cleft of the rock, and will cover you with My hand while I pass by. Then I will take away My hand, and you shall see My back; but My face shall not be seen."

—Exodus 33:12-23

In the story before us we find several themes: grace, adoption, sanctification, perseverance, prayer, and the Rock of Christ. The story demonstrates the importance of trusting the veracity of Scripture.

It would be easy to read this story and cast it off as hopelessly contradictory, were it not for our trust in God's Word. Without the Holy Spirit bidding us to dig beyond a shallow reading we could easily stumble on some apparent contradictions. Without a firm belief that the Scriptures are the inerrant, infallible, sufficient, and authoritative Word of God we could stumble on some apparent inconsistencies.

For instance, in verse 12 we see that Moses had "found grace in (God's) sight." But, Moses said, "if I have found grace in Your sight, show me now Your way, that...I may find grace in Your sight." Did Moses have God's grace already, or was he looking to find it?

The answer is that he had it, but he was having trouble seeing it. Surely, we can relate to that. How many of you are right now saved by grace? How many felt a twinge of doubt when I asked the question? If you are not sure, you are not saved. But even when people are sure of their salvation, it is sometimes a struggle to see its reality because we are saved by faith—not knowledge, nor experience. And "faith is the substance of things hoped for, the evidence of things not seen" (Hebrews 11:1). Faith is not seen! We are saved by what is not seen.

When Moses brought God's law down from the mountain, he found the children of Israel engaged in idol worship, dancing before the Golden Calf. They had just received the law and given themselves in covenant (promised) to God to obey His Word when they forsook that promise before the law was even delivered. Too often God's people are quick to neglect their promises. New Christians are filled with hope and resolve and zealous commitment to follow God's way, only to find themselves compromised and backslidden in short order.

People mistakenly believe that their salvation is dependent upon their own faith and faithfulness. Isn't that what I just said—salvation by faith alone? Yes, but we are not saved by *our* faith, though our faith plays a role in salvation. How could the fickleness of human faithfulness save anyone? People are weak, people are ignorant, people are untrustworthy, people are totally depraved. One day they believe and the next they don't. Human faith is not able to save anyone. Besides, before a person is saved he has no faith, so, how could faith that a person doesn't have save him?

The answer is that people are not saved by their own faith, but by God's faithfulness. God is faithful to His promises. God's faithfulness will not let us down. God is not faithful one day and faithless the next. God is always faithful. We are saved by God's faithfulness to His covenant promises. God will do what He said He would do. If He had no intention of doing it, He would not have said that He would. God's Word does not change. He speaks and it is! This is the faith that saves.

Another way to say it is that we are not saved by mere faith, but by faith in the right thing—the right means, the right end. Faith in Buddha or faith in modern science are not able to save. Only faith in Christ rests upon the faithfulness of God. Salvation in Christ is a promise of God. Salvation in, by, or through any other is not. Only Christ saves because only Christ is the fulfillment of God's promise.

God said He would send a Savior, and He did. Jesus said He will save all who believe, and He will. The question is not whether God will save—He will. The question is not who God will save, He will save all who believe. The only question is, do *you* believe?—not will you believe if and when God saves you, but do you believe *right now*?

Get Real!

The wisdom of the world stands in contradiction to the gospel of Jesus Christ. So often we are told that we must be realistic, meaning that we should adapt to the reality in which we find ourselves. It means that we should understand that reality cannot be changed, but that we must change ourselves and our beliefs to fit into reality. We are told that we must be practical, where being practical means that we must yield to the unchangeableness of some current scientific understanding of reality.

But such practicality—thinking that reality cannot be changed—is not of God. The belief that reality cannot be changed is not true. Christians are not to adjust their beliefs to correspond to an experience of some supposed reality or other. As soon as Christians begin to think that faith in the gospel needs to be adjusted to fit the realities of the modern world, they have fallen into apostasy—unfaithfulness. Christian belief does not need to adjust itself to the realities of the modern world. Rather, Christians need to adjust the so called realities of the modern world to the dictates of Christian belief. Reality is changing all the time, it is God alone who changes not (Malachi 3:6).

When Christianity conquered the Roman empire it did not make adjustments in the gospel in order to appeal to the felt needs of Roman pagans. No, the gospel did not adjust to the realities of the world, the world adjusted to the truth of God's Word. The world is to be changed by the gospel. The gospel is not to be changed by the world.

When the gospel is changed by the world, then there is trouble—false teaching, backsliding, rationalizing, and accommodation. The church is to protect itself from such things, not give herself to them—not for any reason, not to increase membership or budget, not to strengthen or encourage the faithful, nor to reach the lost. Who are we that we can improve the gospel or God's salvation methods? The modern track record to improve God's Word and Way stands as a testimony against such efforts.

Increase

The church is called to be faithful to the gospel that has been entrusted to her. Our job is faithfulness, God's job is increase (1 Corinthians 3:7). When there is no increase we need to examine our faithfulness, not get frustrated with God's lack of responsiveness. The church grows in God's time, according to God's plan, and by God's methods.

Trying to get ahead of God is a well-worn path of sin. It is so easy to get frustrated with God's apparent slowness. But "the Lord is not slack concerning His promise, as some count slackness, but is longsuffering toward us, not willing that any should perish but that all should come to repentance" (2 Peter 3:9).

Have you ever tried to hurry a relationship? Moses said, "Show me now Your way, that I may know You" (Exodus 33:13). Indeed, Moses knew from the beginning that salvation involves a personal relationship with the Lord. Have you ever tried to be a match maker, thinking that two people would make a great couple? Such things cannot be hurried. In fact, they are not really in our control at all. You can introduce people, but beyond that it's out of our hands. Relationships take time, and we mess them up when we try to hurry them along, or force them to conform to our expectations.

When the Israelites were caught in the act of idolatry, God was going to punish them—not by keeping them from the Promised Land, but by absenting His presence from them. God had been leading Israel Himself, by pillar of fire by night and smoke by day. But after the Golden Calf incident He told Moses He would send His Angel to lead them (see Exodus 32:34).

They were commanded to leave Sinai for the Promised Land, but God would not go with them. "Go up to a land flowing with milk and honey; for I will not go up in your midst, lest I consume you on the way, for you are a stiff-necked people" (Exodus 33:3). God was so mad that He thought He might destroy them, so He absented His presence from them.

Leadership

It is at this point that Moses exercised his role as mediator. God chose Moses to lead Israel out of Egypt to the Promised Land. Moses was the leader. His job was to receive God's Word and give it to the people. He was also to pray for the people, to represent the people before God, to work and pray for their salvation. Moses' place of leadership was between God and His people.

Moses' leadership was a basis for the function of the priesthood, mediating between God and His people. We know that this was a temporary function because we know "there is one God and one Mediator between God and men, the Man Christ Jesus" (1 Timothy 2:5). But at that time Moses' role was to mediate.

God had not withdrawn His presence from Moses, only from His people. So Moses argued with God (as he was wont to do). He argued that it had been God's purpose in choosing Israel to make His grace and glory known through them to all people. But if He withdrew His presence from Israel, "how then will it be known that Your people and I have found grace in Your sight, except You go with us?" (Exodus 33:16).

Moses argued that God's purpose would be better fulfilled if God did not withdraw His presence from the people, that God's presence with His people would demonstrate God's reality to the watching world.

At verse 16 there is a connection made between God's presence and the separation of God's people from the world. "So we shall be separate," said Moses, "Your people and I, from all the people who are upon the face of the earth." God's presence (not to be confused with salvation) requires separation from worldly corruption. Corruption chases away God's presence, and God's presence chases away corruption. They are like oil and water. They do not mix.

The application of this doctrine of separation is a key concern today. Do you long for God's presence in your life? Do you feel abandoned by God? Does your life lack the manifest presence of the Lord?

Separation

You may be saved—headed for the Promised Land, and still lack God's presence in your life. If so, you need to talk to the Mediator—not Moses, but Jesus. It may be that you are not sufficiently separated from the world. It may be that you have received Christ, taken your vows of faithfulness, been baptized, but in your weaker moments you still dance before an idol, going along in order to get along in the world.

God didn't take away the Promised Land from the idolatrous Israelites. He took away His presence! Is God's presence lacking in your life? Perhaps you need to separate yourself from sin and temptation.

What sin and temptation? Jesus said, "Do not love the world or the things in the world. If anyone loves the world, the love of the Father is not in him. For all that is in the world—the lust of the flesh, the lust of the eyes, and the pride of life—is not of the Father but is of the world. (1 John 2:15-16). Separate yourselves from the lust of the flesh, the lust of the eyes, and the pride of life.

Avoid what people used to call the seven deadly sins—pride, avarice (or covetousness), envy, wrath, lust, gluttony, and sloth (or laziness). Avoid these and see if God's presence doesn't fill your heart to overflowing!

Pride, covetousness, jealousy, anger, lust, gluttony, and laziness—these are the things that keep God from us.

May 26, 1996

Faith's Reward

Now faith is the substance of things hoped for, the evidence of things not seen. For by it the elders obtained a good testimony. By faith we understand that the worlds were framed by the word of God, so that the things which are seen were not made of things which are visible. By faith Abel offered to God a more excellent sacrifice than Cain, through which he obtained witness that he was righteous, God testifying of his gifts; and through it he being dead still speaks. By faith Enoch was taken away so that he did not see death, "and was not found, because God had taken him"; for before he was taken he had this testimony, that he pleased God. But without faith it is impossible to please Him, for he who comes to God must believe that He is, and that He is a rewarder of those who diligently seek Him. By faith Noah, being divinely warned of things not yet seen, moved with godly fear, prepared an ark for the saving of his household, by which he condemned the world and became heir of the righteousness which is according to faith.

—Hebrews 11:1-7

Chapter eleven of Hebrews begins with a conclusion about justification by faith. Chapter ten presents the argument that the ceremonial law of animal sacrifices has come to an end with the supreme sacrifice of Jesus Christ. If we undervalue the significance of this argument, we will also undervalue the importance of living by faith in Christ.

This discussion of faith is about the end of one system of belief and worship, and the beginning of another. We know that Christ put an end to the practice of animal sacrifices and ceremonial law—the Old Testament forms of worship. But Christ did not simply discontinue the old practices, He brought them to their conclusion, their fulfillment, by His self sacrifice on the cross.

The author of Hebrews argued this logic to convince Old Testament Jews that Jesus Christ was the fulfillment of their own religious hopes. It is important for us to understand that this was not some arbitrary change in worship style, but is the very heart of the New Testament. The New Covenant given by God through faith in Christ requires the belief in Christ as the fulfillment of Old Testament prophecy. Christian worship should reflect this truth.

Christ brought nothing less than a New Covenant with God—yet it is not new at all. It is the heart of the Old Covenant without the ceremonial trappings that anticipated the Messiah. Christ's sacrifice was the fulfillment of the ancient promise that God would send a Savior. The fulfillment of that promise then allowed the foreshadowing aspects of ceremonial law and worship to fall away in order to reveal the fact that the promised Savior had indeed come.

Faith

The writer of Hebrews drew upon the prophecy of Habakkuk to show that the New Covenant was contained within the Old. Habak-kuk prophesied that the Savior would soon come, and in the mean time "the just shall live by faith" (Habakkuk 2:4, Hebrews 10:38). Faith in the *promised* Messiah would provide God's people with everything necessary for salvation until He came. Faith in the promised Messiah would provide justification, righteousness, patience (or longsuffering), and sanctification.

Indeed, the argument went, faith had always been the at heart of God's Covenant with His people. Chapter eleven admirably demonstrates this through a review of Old Testament history and the historic role faith played in the lives of God's people—Abel, Enoch, Noah, Abraham, Sarah, Isaac, Jacob, Joseph, Moses, Joshua, Gideon, Sampson, David, Samuel, and others.

The point is that Chapter eleven begins with a conclusion. It cannot be interpreted as if it stands alone as an abstract description of generic faith. The faith of Hebrews is not generic faith. It is not talking about human faithfulness as if it were a labor of human perseverance. Rather, it is the capstone of a particular faith—faith in Jesus Christ. Not an abstract Christ who dropped out of the sky from nowhere, but Jesus Christ, who is the very fulfillment of the Old Testament itself. There is no Christ other than Jesus Christ, the Savior promised by God in the

Old Testament. Nor any saving faith other than faith in the faithfulness of God in Christ.

It is so easy to pluck the first verse of chapter eleven out of its context and begin to imagine all sorts of unwarranted things about faith. "Now faith is the substance of things hoped for, the evidence of things not seen" (Hebrews 11:1). The greatest error related to this notion of faith is to turn it into a labor of righteousness, a matter of human effort. People imagine that the work of faith is like pulling one's self up by the bootstraps and persevering to the end. The perseverance part is fine, but Christian faith is not a matter of self effort. There is effort in faithfulness, of course. But its source is not self, but God. God works His faith in His people.

Wrong

The false belief of self-effort leads people to think that if they believe hard enough, if they pray long enough, if they go to church often enough, then God will grant them their wishes, as if God is a great spiritual vending machine in the sky. Put in your effort, press the right buttons, and presto!

Similarly, people mistakenly believe that God will necessarily heal them if only they have enough faith. And, conversely, that the lack of healing indicates a lack of faith. People mistakenly think that they don't measure up because God didn't heal their cancer—or whatever. Well, people don't measure up, but it has nothing to do with cancer.

People carry this kind of false belief even further by thinking that God has punished them by inflicting them with some illness, or by the death of a loved one. It is so tempting and easy to engage in this kind of self pity. There is a sense in which self pity is satisfying. It builds the ego by strengthening the walls that separate people from God by pitting God against them. People like to feel sorry for themselves because God is so unmerciful, and they are so helpless.

But such pitiful self indulgence reveals nothing about God. And it ignores the help that God sent in Christ. Self-pity works by misappropriating the natural feelings associated with illness and loss to increase sorrow and self-concern, thus coalescing our godless and graceless sense of self. "Poor me," people cry, "Why did God forsake me?" The normal pain of illness and loss is used to cut people away from God, rather than draw them into a healing and saving relationship with Him by making them think that He has abandoned them.

Again, the faith that saves is not *our* faith—as if we could be faithful enough to merit salvation. No, we do not deserve salvation. Rather, people are saved by grace through faith in Christ—through His faithfulness, through His sacrifice on the cross. We are saved by grace through our faith in Christ, but not because of our own faithfulness.

Salvation comes only because of the faithfulness of God in Christ. His faithfulness saves, and we share in His salvation because of our trust in the faithfulness of Christ—in spite of our own faithlessness. No one is worthy to be saved. No one is faithful enough to warrant salvation. People are saved because of Christ's faith and God's mercy, and that alone.

Neither are people healed because of their worthiness. People are not healed because they have enough faith to receive God's healing. We must realize that physical healing and eternal salvation are not the same, that there is no correlation between physical healing and eternal salvation. Jesus used physical healing as a way to teach about eternal salvation—that's all. Not all who were healed were saved. Remember the ten lepers in Luke 17:17. Nor were all who were saved healed. Remember Paul's thorn (2 Corinthians 12:7).

Those who are saved suffer the consequences of life in this fallen world just as do those who are not saved. Salvation preserves no one from illness and disease. Nor is salvation a defense against the slings and arrows of God's enemies. In fact, the saved often come under increased attack. The history of the church is littered with the mutilated corpses of the faithful. Suffering and hardship often accompany salvation.

Yet, there is a relationship between health and religious practice. Paul writes, "For he who eats and drinks in an unworthy manner"—he is discussing communion here—"eats and drinks judgment to himself, not discerning the Lord's body. For this reason many are weak and sick among you, and many sleep" (1 Corinthians 11:29-30).

Paul suggests here that the improper administration of Holy Communion can result in the malfunction of the body. Weakness and sickness can result from improper communion with Christ Jesus. The weakness and sickness alluded to can manifest in the church, in the body of Christ, and/or in the physical bodies of individuals.

But it is not the lack of faith that brings such a consequence. It is poor administration. There is no lack in the saving faithfulness of Christ. Rather, the failure to live by faith, ignoring Christ's faithfulness, is the failure to rely upon the Holy Spirit. Unregenerate people cannot enjoy the blessings of the Holy Spirit. God's blessings are not necessarily the health and strength of an individual body, but are always the health and strength of Christ's eternal body.

The martyrs enjoyed the health and strength of the Holy Spirit, but they suffered greatly. The strength of the Holy Spirit shines all the more brightly in the weakness of God's people. God has always chosen the weak and infirm in which to manifest his power and glory. May we be weak enough for God's glory to shine in our lives!

The rewards of faithfulness are not rewards at all according to worldly standards. Success in God's eyes—faithfulness—seldom brings success by worldly measures. Faithfulness has no concern for worldly measures. Faithfulness lobbies neither for nor against worldly success. But neither does God adapt salvation to conform to the standards of worldly success and health. Rather, God dictates different standards of success for His faithful people.

Take some time and evaluate your success against God's standards. How have worldly measures of success effected your spiritual life? How have they shaped your understanding of salvation? How have they shaped your expectations of your church? What is the measure of a faithful life? What is the measure of a faithful church?

June 2, 1996

Redemption

In Him we have redemption through His blood, the forgiveness of sins, according to the riches of His grace which He made to abound toward us in all wisdom and prudence, having made known to us the mystery of His will, according to His good pleasure which He purposed in Himself, that in the dispensation of the fullness of the times He might gather together in one all things in Christ, both which are in heaven and which are on earth—in Him. In Him also we have obtained an inheritance, being predestined according to the purpose of Him who works all things according to the counsel of His will, that we who first trusted in Christ should be to the praise of His glory.

—Ephesians 1:7-12

Redemption is a trade. One thing is redeemed or traded for another. In days gone by Green Stamps were traded in at the Redemption Center for something of greater value. Our redemption by the blood of Christ and the forgiveness of sins because of God's overflowing grace and mercy is just a simple trade. Your life for His. Your old sinful life is traded in for new life in Christ. His life for yours.

Does it sound too easy? This divine trade is a lot of things, but easy is not one of them. It sounds easy because it is a very simple idea. It is an easy idea to understand. But it is not easy to do because there is nothing that you or I can do to make it happen. No matter how smart, or how strong, or how rich, or how well connected in society we are, we cannot have any effect upon God's redemption. God not only redeems when He chooses, but whom He chooses. And there is nothing we can do about it. So, I say that it is not easy because it doesn't even fall in the category of human doing. We think of "easy" as being easy to do. But in this case we can't do anything about it.

But neither is it hard, for the same reasons. God does it all, so from our perspective it is not hard for us, either. We can do nothing about it. Consequently, it isn't "hard" at all. Nor is it "easy." These categories do not apply. It does not fall into the easy/hard continuum.

Kick Back And Let God

So, does this mean that we can just kick back and let God do it all? Heaven forbid! The reality is precisely the opposite. Because redemption is not something that we do, and because God provides redemption for "whosoever believes in him" (John 3:16), those who simply believe are redeemed already. They are not redeemed because they believe, they believe because they are redeemed.

Sometimes it seems like there is something that we have to do in order to receive God's redemption, but such thinking is wrong. There is nothing we can do! Redemption is all God's doing, and in fact, it has already been done for those who believe. So this "believing" is not a function of human ability, will, or understanding. It is, rather, a passive receiving.

If I want to give you a nickel, all you have to do is receive it. You don't have to want it. You don't have to understand it. You don't have to earn it. Just hold out your hand and receive it.

"So," you say, "there is something I have to do after all. I have to hold out my hand." Don't be silly. You don't have to hold out your hand. I'll leave it on your pew or your back porch. You don't have to do anything to get it. It's yours. But, of course, if you don't believe that its yours, you won't bother to receive it.

The grace of God's redemption is like that nickel—except that it's a priceless diamond, not a nickel. The giving of it has already been accomplished. It already belongs to those who believe that it's true. Just go down to the redemption center and pick it up.

Now, once you believe that God's forgiveness, salvation, and redemption are true—that is, if you really believe—you will live your life on the basis of that belief. And if you don't actually live your life by it, then you don't really believe it—because if you believed it, you'd live it.

I'm not trying to get fancy with my words. I'm trying to show you that this is an argument "by definition." If you understand the definition of the world *believe*, then you know that belief is not just something mental, but it has actual, physical elements to it. It's not just mental, but it has physical components.

Nice Church

The purpose of God's redemption is not for us to have a nice little church, where everyone enjoys the Sunday lecture, and goes away comfortable and unchanged. Our purpose is not to simply grow old together—although I hope and pray that we will grow old together. Rather, our purpose is to do something because of our redemption—assuming, of course, that you believe that you are in fact redeemed by Jesus Christ.

If this church is like most churches—and it seems to be, then there are a variety of people involved. Some are born again and on fire for the Lord, others are unregenerate, and everything in between.

It seems to me that in general we could say that the fires of regeneracy and passion for Christ have grown cold at this church (like they have in so many churches) over the past few years. And that the church is in need of renewal. Anyone who wants renewal or revival believes that they need a movement of the Holy Spirit because they do not currently have a movement of the Holy Spirit. I don't think anyone would argue about that. If you already have it, why would you still want it?

I'm talking about the church here. The church is recovering from some hard times, is it not? But when we talk about the church, we are not talking about the building. We are talking about the people. And although we mean all the people, we also mean each individual person. If the church is in need of renewal, then the people need renewal—you and I.

The present danger for this church (or any church) is to think that the pastor is going to make it all better. It's a mistake to think that renewed passion for Christ is my responsibility. I'm not trying to shirk my responsibility for leadership, I'm trying to tell you that any renewal that may come must come from the people involved. I'm already renewed. Are you? I've crossed my Rubicon. I've burned the bridges behind me. I've left the apostasy of liberalism and have no interest in retiring in its comforts. The danger before you today is to think that this church is going to go back together like it used to be—whatever that may have been. Or to be just like it used to be only bigger.

Used To Be

We must understand that nothing is ever like it used to be. It never was like we think it used to be! This church will never be like it used to be. It will either be renewed by the power of Christ—you will be renewed, redeemed, changed—or it will die the death of liberalism—you will die the death of liberalism. We are today teetering on the precipice. You are teetering on the precipice between renewal and slow death—and everybody knows it. But nobody wants to talk about it because it is a painful reality.

So, my question for you is: Are you redeemed by the blood of Christ? If you are, you graduate to a life of service in the Lord. If you aren't, you have misunderstood something and need to reevaluate your life. I'm not going to make the difference here. If there is any difference to be made, Jesus Christ will make it. If you think that I can make this church just the way that you like it, just the way it used to be, you are sadly mistaken.

We can do nothing to receive redemption. But once it is received we must do everything we can because we have received it. Works of righteousness are not and cannot be done in order to receive salvation or redemption or forgiveness. It is an issue of motivation. Why do you do what you do? If you are trying to do things to get God to give you salvation, you are in trouble because it will never happen. You will die in your good works and go to hell. There is only one way to go to heaven and that is by the blood of Christ.

Those who have already received redemption by the blood of Christ are free from the rat race of trying to impress God, and are empowered to do works of mercy and righteousness in Christ. The difference is that unredeemed people work to impress God, while it is God Himself who works through the redeemed by the power of His Holy Spirit.

No Middle Ground

Notice that there is no middle ground here. It's redeemed or unredeemed. The blood of Christ is a great divide, a great divide in history and a great divide in humanity. But it should not be a divide in the church. Everyone in the church should be on the right side of redemption. This is the church unity issue. Everything the unredeemed do displeases God, and everything done in Christ by the redeemed pleases God—only because it is Christ doing it.

The application of this important teaching is twofold: 1) do nothing to try to impress God. Simply receive God's forgiveness, salvation, and redemption. And 2) do everything because you believe, love, and trust God's redemption by the blood of Christ. Be the person God wants you to be, all the time.

The first area of application is prayer and Bible study. If you are not involved in regular prayer and Bible study you will fail to understand and apply God's Word to your life. I said regular prayer and Bible study. Do you think I mean Christmas and Easter? Of course I do, but not that alone. Do you think I mean monthly attendance at church. Certainly, but if that's all you're doing, you have missed the boat. Do you think I mean weekly prayer and Bible study? Of course, but if you think I mean that attending worship once a week qualifies for prayer and Bible study, you are mistaken.

Sunday morning worship is not your prayer and Bible study time. It's mine! On Sunday mornings I share my study of God's Word and I engage His Holy Spirit in prayer. Sunday School teachers do the same. But for the most part you only listen. You are not engaged. Listening to someone talk about God is not the same as engaging God yourself.

It is my hope that you will learn from me, that you will do as I do. You don't have to get up and preach, but you must study the Scriptures for yourselves, and personally engage the Holy Spirit in prayer. My purpose as your pastor is not to entertain you, but to teach you by example. My purpose as your pastor is to encourage you forward in your faith, to warn you of spiritual dangers, and to admonish your spiritual laziness.

The application related to God's redemption, no matter which side of redemption you may be on, is to take up your Bible and follow me in study and prayer. That's the first step.

(At the conclusion of this service people were invited forward to pray and more than half of the congregation came forward.)

June 9, 1996

God The Father

Therefore gird up the loins of your mind, be sober, and rest your hope fully upon the grace that is to be brought to you at the revelation of Jesus Christ; as obedient children, not conforming yourselves to the former lusts, as in your ignorance; but as He who called you is holy, you also be holy in all your conduct, because it is written, "Be holy, for I am holy." And if you call on the Father, who without partiality judges according to each one's work, conduct yourselves throughout the time of your stay here in fear; knowing that you were not redeemed with corruptible things, like silver or gold, from your aimless conduct received by tradition from your fathers, but with the precious blood of Christ, as of a lamb without blemish and without spot. He indeed was foreordained before the foundation of the world, but was manifest in these last times for you who through Him believe in God, who raised Him from the dead and gave Him glory, so that your faith and hope are in God.

—1 Peter 1:13-21

I have spent many hours thinking about what happened here last week. Like many of you I stand in awe and thanksgiving for the outpouring of God's Holy Spirit, and the forgiveness and opportunities for new beginnings that come with God's grace. I am thankful for God's invitation to forgiveness and newness of life.

I am also deeply concerned about what happened. I am aware of the dangers of misinterpretation and misappropriation that accompany the movement of God's Spirit. There has never been a time in history that renewal and revival was not accompanied by the dangers of misunderstanding and misuse. Consequently, this is not a time for us to kick back and bask in the light of God's glory—though we should certainly give our full attention to God's grace and glory. But, rather than resting on our laurels, we need to give ourselves to the hard work of sanctification and growth in grace and holiness.

Following

Like the Israelites in the wilderness following God's pillar of smoke by day and pillar of fire by night, once we have begun our journey, we must move when God moves and rest when God rests. To rest when God moves or to move when God rests provides opportunities for Satan to attack. Because God is our protection we must stay near to Him, following wherever He leads.

When people begin to follow God or to follow God more closely Satan will also move to counter their movement toward God. The more effective you become as a servant of God, the more Satan will target you and try to interfere with your faith and effectiveness. One sure way to incur the wrath of Satan is to receive God's grace and endeavor to live a life of faithfulness.

I am also confused about what happened here last week, because not just one thing happened. Many things happened. As many things happened as there were people present. God works in the lives of individuals. Consequently, each individual will have had a different experience or take on it. And that is as it should be. That's the way God works.

Let me also say a few words about growth in general. Growth comes in spurts. There are times of intense growth activity and times of quiet assimilation. This pattern is both natural and normal in everything that grows. In the biological process of cell division, producing cellular growth, or the awkwardness of adolescence, we see this pattern of quiet assimilation and rapid growth.

In the excitement of setting our opportunity for renewal in visible relief I may have obscured the fact that the fruits of ministry generally have a long life cycle, certainly longer than six or eight weeks. Therefore, the ministry of every pastor is deeply dependent upon the ministry of his predecessor. Pastors reap what others have planted. Seldom do they harvest their own seed.

The seed blooming at this church today was not planted by me but by those who labored before me. There are ministries of plowing, planting, and harvesting, and their are appropriate seasons for each ministry. One season cannot begrudge another, nor one ministry another. While plowing is a time of upheaval, seed time is quiet and still, and harvest is a time of bounty. All are equally necessary.

But we must remember that no matter what our ministry—plowing, planting, or harvesting—it is God who provides the increase. We cannot make anything grow. We can only be faithful to the ministry of our season.

Application

Peter calls God's people to the task of living in God's presence. Once God is revealed and experienced, then the discipline of daily living in God's presence must be engaged. While there are certain practicalities involved with living in God's presence, we must not be too hasty in turning God's revelation into a practical application. People are not saved by practical application, but by the grace of God.

People usually mean by the word *application* the right application of the right thing. To apply the wrong thing, or to apply the right thing in the wrong way will not get the job done. In religion the thing that is to be applied is belief. Christian belief is the fountain of Christian action. To base action upon wrong belief leads to wrong action. Similarly, to apply right belief in the wrong way will lead to error and heartache. Consequently, we must spend some time determining and confirming our beliefs in the light of God's revelation. To do otherwise is to put the proverbial cart before the horse.

Peter said, "gird up the loins of your mind, be sober" (1 Peter 1:13) Peter calls God's people to prepare themselves for some hard thinking that will require clarity, discipline, and discernment. But he also calls them to build their understanding upon the foundation of God's revelation, not upon their personal experience of God. We must begin with the grace of God's revelation in Jesus Christ, not with our personal experience of God. The difference is critical. One way assumes the truth of God's Word, the other assumes the truth of human experience.

The assumptions we make are critical to the outworking of our faith. Our assumptions and beliefs determine the course and character of our spiritual life. One is a narrow way determined by God, the other is a broad way determined by the opinions of men. So, Peter counsels, set your course on God's way, not your own. Begin with God's Word, trust God's Word, not your personal experience.

Proverbs 14:12 reads, "There is a way that seems right to a man, But its end is the way of death." It is so important that it is repeated in Proverbs 16:25. The ancient gospel writer of Proverbs warns God's people about trusting in their own experiences. This is a critical lesson for us right now. Don't discount your personal experience, but don't rely upon it either.

Faith In...

A personal relationship with the Lord of glory is absolutely essential. But we do not have faith in our personal relationship. We have faith in Christ alone. Children may have a personal relationship with a pet—a dog or a cat. And that personal relationship may be very enjoyable, but it cannot be the basis upon which to worship dogs or cats. The ancient Egyptians fell in love with personal relationship itself and in their carelessness they ended up worshiping cats.

The danger here is to make personal relationship the ground or condition of worship. To do so is an error. People have personal relationships with all kinds of things which are not worthy of worship—trees, rocks, animals, and other people. And people have erred by worshiping things rather than God.

God establishes personal relationship with His people by means of His personal revelation in, through, and by His Son, Jesus Christ. The point is simply that He establishes it on the basis of His revelation. We don't establish it, He does. Our role is that of respondent, not initiator.

Our personal relationship with God produces many things, among them are sanctification and evangelism—growth and outreach. Peter remarks about the proper ordering of these things. First, comes separation for sanctification. God calls us apart from the world, to separate ourselves from its desires and influences. God calls His people to purity and holiness.

God wants us to clean up our act, but God also knows that all human beings are totally depraved—immoral in and of themselves. People are unable to be good, or righteous, or holy without the presence and power of God's Holy Spirit.

Not only are people hopelessly lost in and of themselves—without Christ, but people do not complete their course in morality in this life. No Christian is able to ever say that he or she has arrived at any kind of moral superiority. Quite the contrary, the greatest saints find that the closer their relationship with God becomes, the more convicted and convinced they become of their own inferiority to the moral standard set by Christ.

Christians are not to conform to their former lusts and desires of the world. Peter, quoting God's law in Leviticus (11:44-45), said, "Be holy, for I am holy." The words belong to God and are applicable to people of both the Old and New Testaments. Paul said it this way, "do not be conformed to this world, but be transformed by the renewing of your mind, that you may prove what is that good and acceptable and perfect will of God" (Romans 12:2).

Men

I need to say something to fathers this morning because fathers—husbands and men—play a key role in God's redemption plan. First, the whole purpose of redemption is wrapped up in fatherhood itself. Malachi, the last book of the Old Testament, says in its last verses, "Remember the Law of Moses, My servant, Which I commanded him in Horeb for all Israel, With the statutes and judgments. Behold, I will send you Elijah the prophet Before the coming of the great and dreadful day of the Lord. And he will turn The hearts of the fathers to the children, And the hearts of the children to their fathers...." That is the mandate for the New Testament.

When Adam fell the family also fell out of proper relationship with God through sin. God intends to restore that relationship through reconciliation by the blood of Christ. And God's point man for family reconciliation—the reestablishment of God's authority and order—is the husband/father. But we must also be aware that God's order and authority (Ephesians 5-6) does not establish a pecking order of superiority. Remember that God has reversed human values. God's ways are not our ways.

Jesus said it this way, "You know that the rulers of the Gentiles lord it over them, and those who are great exercise authority over them. Yet it shall not be so among you; but whoever desires to become great among you, let him be your servant" (Matthew 20:25-26). To be in line with God's order of authority is not to be on the top of the dog pile, but on the bottom. It is to choose to be on the bottom as a matter of service to the Lord.

The same should be true of Christian families. Christian fathers do not lord it over their wives and children, but serve their best interests. A Christian father husbands his wife and children. To husband means "to direct and manage with frugality." This is the responsibility that God has given to husbands. Husbandry is the management of domestic affairs and resources. It is a domestic art.

Modern families have goofed up God's order. Today, the men work and play outside the home and the women husband the family. The women direct and manage the affairs of modern families. Everyone knows that there are serious problems with our families. We hear much talk about the breakdown or crisis of the family. Families are falling apart. They are not working.

Alcoholism, immorality, incest, and abuse are rampant. Children are disobedient and unruly. Many modern people see these things as family problems and are looking for solutions. But Scripture suggests a different take on the situation. Scripture suggests that these things—alcoholism, immorality, incest, abuse, disobedience, etc.—are not problems, but symptoms. And as long as Christians continue to address the symptoms of family breakdown and ignore the underlying causes, they will continue to suffer from the disease.

The underlying cause, according to Scripture, is the improper administration of God's authority in the family. The lines of authority and responsibility are all messed up and as long as they stay messed up the problems—symptoms—will persist.

That's a whole other sermon—even a series of sermons. But the point this morning is that the buck stops—and begins—with the men, with husbands and fathers. We men must be reconciled in our relationship with God through the blood of Christ, and reclaim our rightful place in our own households. That rightful place being the head, wielding God's upside-down authority.

According to God's order the head is the chief servant of the well-being of those under his authority. The head of the household is not to relinquish his authority or responsibility to someone else—not even his wife! Nor is he to lord it over his family!

Begin Here

What does all of this mean? I don't know. I've never experienced such a thing. But I know that it begins and ends with Christ. It hinges upon our personal relationship with Jesus Christ as Lord and Savior. That is the place to begin. We men desperately need to confess and profess our faith in Christ in our families, to our families, with our families. We need to let our wives and children see that Christ is our head. We must model submissiveness to the headship of Christ.

The importance of doing this in our families cannot be under estimated. It is not only important for our families to hear it from us, it is important for us to show and tell Christ's leadership. It is important because we cannot fool our families about our relationship with the Lord. We live with them. They know when we are telling the truth and when we are not. They know when our actions betray our words. And consequently, they will keep us honest.

Won't you commit or recommit yourself to reconciliation in Christ, and start a fresh page of your family history today?

June 16, 1996

God The Son

And if you call on the Father, who without partiality judges according to each one's work, conduct yourselves throughout the time of your stay here in fear; knowing that you were not redeemed with corruptible things, like silver or gold, from your aimless conduct received by tradition from your fathers, but with the precious blood of Christ, as of a lamb without blemish and without spot. He indeed was foreordained before the foundation of the world, but was manifest in these last times for you who through Him believe in God, who raised Him from the dead and gave Him glory, so that your faith and hope are in God. —*1 Peter 1:17-21*

The appearance of Jesus Christ was the critical event in salvation history. Jesus Christ, second person of the Trinity, Son of God and Son of Man, is a watershed, who determines and divides the course of history. A watershed causes part of the water to flow in one direction and part to flow in another. Jesus Christ is a watershed, and not an accidental watershed, but "foreordained before the foundation of the world" (1 Peter 1:20).

Most evangelical statements of faith confess that we believe that there is one God, eternally existent in three persons: Father, Son and Holy Ghost. We also believe in the deity of Christ. These things are common to all Christians. Where these things are not believed and confessed, Christianity is not present. Beliefs determine actions, and actions reveal beliefs.

Jesus Christ effectively divides the people of the world into two categories: those who are faithful, and those who are not. This is because Jesus is the only way of salvation, and there are those who accept this fact and those who reject or ignore it.

Orthodoxy

The determination of the correct teaching (orthodox doctrine) of Jesus Christ is a matter of much confusion and misunderstanding in the history of the church. Not because it is difficult, but because Satan has counterfeited the gospel. Yet, true faith can only be built upon the right understanding of the correct teaching. So, it is necessary for God's people to claim the orthodox, historically affirmed teaching of Jesus Christ.

Over the long course of history there have been many debates about Christian beliefs, and the essential Christian beliefs have been identified. The historical witness is built upon the foundational beliefs agreed upon by historic Protestant, Evangelical, Reformed churches. Part of our understanding is that Christianity did not begin with the New Testament, nor with the Reformation, but began with God and His purpose for creating the world in the first place. We believe that all of history is Christian history and that all of it is used by God to fulfill His promise of salvation in Christ.

Children, how do you know what is true/false? You trust your parents.

When the Department of the Treasury teaches its agents to identify counterfeit currency it instructs them in the marks of authentic currency. Counterfeit bills are like real bills, except for only one or two details. The differences are barely noticeable to the untrained eye, yet they are critical. Rather than focusing on all the known variations of counterfeit bills, agents learn to identify the real thing. Any bills that vary from the marks of the original are counterfeit.

This methodology is useful in theology as well because Satan deceives by counterfeiting God's truth. Counterfeit currency has no real value. There is nothing to back it up. It pretends to be something it is not. It is worthless because it is not authorized. It looks like the real thing, but is not. There are many ways to counterfeit something, but only one authentic, authoritative way to make the genuine article.

The critical teaching about God the Son, manifest in Jesus Christ, is that Jesus is "of one substance and equal with the Father" (Westminster Confession, 8.2). Jesus is God Himself. The two traditional errors regarding Christ are an over emphasis of Christ's divinity to the point of denying or overshadowing His humanity. And the opposite—an over emphasis of Christ's humanity to the point of denying or overshadowing His divinity.

The common faith proclaims that Christ is both divine and human at the same time, without mixing or losing sight of or diminishing the full reality of either of these characteristics. There is a tension or balance that must be maintained for a saving knowledge and a fruitful understanding of Christ.

Heresy

An additional difficulty for the modern religious landscape is that all historical heresies are represented in the current religious scene. Although heretical teachings were identified as corrupt many centuries ago, they never died out completely, but have grown and multiplied over the centuries. They are with us still.

Think of the truth of Christ as a vegetable garden. It is threatened not by one weed, but by many different kinds of weeds—and not weeds only, but bugs, birds, animals, and fungus as well. God's truth has many enemies, but only one defender—Jesus Christ. The only way to have a fruitful garden is by constant attention and nurture. You must not only water, but fence, weed, and watch as well. So it is with God's truth.

Through the dissemination of counterfeit Christianity, Christ's enemies have become very entrenched in the modern world, occupying many centers of financial and political power—even ecclesiastical power. Satan's strongholds are many and well defended, in the church and out. The fact that people find it difficult to believe that Satan works within Christ's churches is a sure sign of Satan's success because Scripture itself tells us that false teaching had invaded the church from the beginning (Jude). Christians have never been protected from Satan by simply belonging to the right institution.

The name of Christ is a mighty spiritual weapon in the battle for God's truth. The name is mighty because it belongs to the Lord of Glory. But when we apply the name of Christ to human institutions we expose ourselves to the possibilities of deceit and error. Perhaps the most readily identifiable of the counterfeit Christian groups are Mormons and Jehovah's Witnesses. Both claim to believe in Christ, but redefine Christ to fit into their respective theologies—theologies not grounded in the whole counsel of God's Word alone.

But before we sling mud at others we need to examine our own eyes for planks (Luke 6:42). If you have never encountered any false beliefs in your own understanding, you must be a candidate for sainthood, or self-deluded, or unconcerned about God's truth. Let's look at each possibility.

Sainthood

First, candidates for sainthood should realize that they are potential founders of new religions and/or sects. Joseph Smith is the patron saint of Mormons, and C.T. Russell and J.F. Rutherford of Jehovah's Witnesses. Every sect, every deviation from the common faith rests upon the teaching of someone who is looked upon as a saint.

In contrast, authentic Christianity is not based upon the teaching of the saints, but upon the teaching of Jesus Christ as found in God's Word. God doesn't need people to interpret and define His Word for others. Scripture interprets and defines Scripture through the teaching agency of the Holy Spirit (1 John 2:27).

God's Word is not only inspired, inerrant, infallible, authoritative, as most evangelical statements of faith proclaim, but it is sufficient as well. Scripture is all we need. However, just because Scripture is all we need, does not mean that we should ignore the witness of history. Many faithful Christians have gone before us, and while their works are not as authoritative as Scripture, they are often helpful and edifying to God's people.

I call you, not to my interpretation of Scripture, but to an understanding of God's Word that is consistent with the historic witness of the church throughout the ages. In that tradition are many voices and many faithful perspectives that will help you steer a faithful course through this perishing world of sin and heartache.

The Holy Spirit has faithfully led the church throughout the ages and will lead you faithfully today by faith in Christ through prayer and study. The Spirit's leadership comes through Bible study and is confirmed through study of the faithful witness of the church (see 2 Timothy 2:15, KJV).

Self-Delusion

The second category of error is self-delusion. The most common sources of self-delusion are ignorance of Christ and ignorance of history. Those who ignore Christ are unable to understand the truth of history because Christ is the Truth of history, where history is understood as His (God's) story. Christ is the watershed of history, and to fail to see that fact is to fail to understand the flow of history.

Included in this category of self-delusion are liberals, who have history but not Christ, and fundamentalists, who have Christ but not history. The fact that liberals reject Jesus Christ is readily apparent. It is more difficult to see that fundamentalists reject history—mostly because so many Christians shun history themselves. They see that history is the playground of liberals. And not wanting to be contaminated with liberalism, they avoid history. And having avoided it, they are unaware of its importance.

Fundamentalists are interested in reestablishing a kind of First Century Christianity by allowing the Holy Spirit to speak to them directly from Scripture (often from only the New Testament as if it can stand alone, apart from its context in the Old Testament), apart from the historical witness of the church. Fundamentalists think that they don't need biblical commentaries because they want God's Word, not man's interpretation.

"Just give me the Bible," they say, "and the Holy Spirit will lead me"—forgetting that they, too, are fallible men. The witness of history shows that this is a well-worn path to heresy. All of the sectarian saints began on this path. While Scripture is sufficient, the testimony of history is helpful. Because Jesus Christ is the Lord of history, ignorance of history is a handicap. There is no reason that Christians should not learn from the faithful witness of those who have gone before them.

The advantage of historical testimony—proven commentaries from the past—is that they have stood the test of time. It is not modern scholarship that should guide the church, but faithful, historic witness. It is God's unchanging truth that will lead the church faithfully, not the whims of scholarly or popular opinion. But this is not to disparage scholarship, but only to make it subservient to Scripture and the historic testimony of the church.

You know that I am not a liberal. Know also that I am not a fundamentalist. The historic witness of faithful Christians does not carry the same authority of Scripture, but it does carry some authority. Nor is it superior to Scripture. Rather, the historic witness is of secondary importance, which means that it is second only to the authority of Scripture. God is not calling today for First Century faithfulness, but for 21st Century faithfulness. History does not run backwards and it is folly to try to recreate some imagined past.

Unconcerned

The third category I mentioned is composed of the unconcerned. It may seem odd that I include the unconcerned as a category of theological error because they aren't even playing the game. How could those who don't care be wrong? They are wrong precisely because they don't care, because there is only one way of salvation, and they don't care about it. They are like drunk drivers who don't care about the law, or the safety of the community. The lack of care is the problem!

Because they don't care about salvation or the blessings of the Holy Spirit they cannot receive them. They will not receive the protection of Jesus Christ, but will be exposed to the wrath of God and the evils of Satan. Not only will they find their way to hell, but their lives will be miserable in the mean time, even if they pretend to be happy. They will waste away, pursuing the empty dreams and illusive fantasies of this perishing world, thinking that that is all there is.

At the present time, people are not so deceived by the evils of anti-Christian sentiment, as they are consumed by the false objectivity that has no concern for the things of Christ. The danger of complacency on the part of the faithful during such a time is that the one leads to the other. It is only a matter of time before the carelessness of the Christless turns into hatred of the faithful.

The danger we face from the ranks of the unconcerned is that when people cease to care for the things of Christ, Christ ceases to care for them (Romans 1:28-32). God enacts a program of tough love. His love and care don't actually stop, but God turns the careless over to suffer the evils of their carelessness in order to help some of them see their need for Jesus.

The growing popularity of religious carelessness threatens the safety of all. The difficult job of the faithful is to help the careless care, to help them see their need to care. The ongoing mission of Jesus Christ, the Son of God, is the incarnation of God's love in a world that doesn't care. It is the mission of Christ, and the mission of His people.

June 23, 1996

When Nations Stumble

Therefore it is also contained in the Scripture, "Behold, I lay in Zion A chief cornerstone, elect, precious, And he who believes on Him will by no means be put to shame." Therefore, to you who believe, He is precious; but to those who are disobedient, "The stone which the builders rejected Has become the chief cornerstone," and "A stone of stumbling And a rock of offense." They stumble, being disobedient to the word, to which they also were appointed. But you are a chosen generation, a royal priesthood, a holy nation, His own special people, that you may proclaim the praises of Him who called you out of darkness into His marvelous light; who once were not a people but are now the people of God, who had not obtained mercy but now have obtained mercy. Beloved, I beg you as sojourners and pilgrims, abstain from fleshly lusts which war against the soul, having your conduct honorable among the Gentiles, that when they speak against you as evildoers, they may, by your good works which they observe, glorify God in the day of visitation. —*1 Peter 2:6-12*

Peter has been arguing that Jesus Christ is the foundation for the dreaded Day of the Lord. Jesus Christ is the fulcrum (or lever) of God's judgment. The cause of Christ will bring God's judgment, but the faithful need not fear because they are covered by the mercy of Christ's blood.

Christ is the cornerstone of God's eternal church. The cornerstone is the stone or brick that is used as a measurement to insure that the rest of the building will be square. The house is built upon a foundation, and the foundation is measured in reference to the cornerstone. The cornerstone establishes the strength and stability of the foundation.

Therefore, said Peter, Jesus is precious to those who believe. But to the disobedient Jesus is a stumbling block, a stone of a different kind. With Jesus Christ set as the reference upon which to build, those who are in line with Jesus are incorporated into the structure (the church), but those who refuse to be set in place in reference to Christ are rejected. They are out of proper alignment.

Israel

The leaders of the Old Testament church of Jerusalem refused to recognize Christ as the cornerstone of the foundation of God's eternal church. And rightly so, because He was not the foundation upon which they had built. They had built the Old Testament church upon the law, not upon grace. They had failed to see that Old Testament law itself was built upon the foundation of God's grace.

They understood themselves to be God's chosen people, special people who had been chosen by God. And indeed they were, but they were not chosen because of a superior blood line. God has adamantly refused to acknowledge any superiority with regard to blood or birth. But over the centuries the Jews had mistakenly attached the idea of their election to the blood and birth heritage of the Jewish nation. They had mistakenly married the kingdom of God with the Jewish state.

The Jewish nation today perpetuates this error in that the Jews persist in trusting in their bloodline rather than in Jesus Christ, the eternal Messiah of God. I am not arguing against the fact that God has a special place and purpose for the Jewish nation. He does. God intends that the world learn from them when they have it right, and when they have it wrong. The Jewish nation continues to serve as a barometer of God's grace and of God's wrath.

The salvation offered by the grace of God through Jesus Christ is not only a watershed, but a stumbling stone. People who are content in themselves take offense at God's salvation offer. Why? Because in order to receive God's offer people must admit that they are hopelessly lost and unable to help themselves. And hopelessly lost people are not content in themselves. The question, "Are you saved?" carries with it the implication that "You are lost." And people don't like to be told that they are lost. (What man on a trip in an unfamiliar area will ever admit that he is lost!)

The appearance of Jesus carries with it the announcement that the world is wrong, mistaken, confused and bound for hell. People content with the world don't like to hear that. They take offense at it.

WRONG!

Offended at the implication that they are wrong and unable to correct themselves, they reject Christ. But notice that in the latter part of verse 8 Peter says that their rejection of Christ is also part of God's plan. Those who reject Christ, who are disobedient to God's Word, have been appointed by God to the path of disobedience, rejection, and destruction (see Romans 9:22).

The glory of God will be demonstrated by the destruction of the faithless, just as the glory of God will be demonstrated by the salvation of the faithful. Both paths reveal and teach the glory of God's sovereignty. God is in charge. God calls all the shots. Everything serves the glory of God.

Consequently, the preaching of salvation in Christ brings about a personal crisis in all who hear it. The rub is that the preaching of the gospel brings salvation to all who will believe, but damnation to those who will not—all to the glory of God. This is the offense of Christ to the ungodly.

But, says Peter to the church, "you are a chosen generation, a royal priesthood, a holy nation" (1 Peter 2:10). Peter was not talking to those who are a nation by blood and birth, but to those who have been adopted into the family of God by grace. The adopted family of God is the basis of God's holy nation. There is no Christian birth right. No one is a Christian by birth. No one was born a Christian. Christians are adopted—born again, not simply born as babies into God's family.

Peter is not talking about a nation with geographical boundaries, but a nation with belief boundaries, faith boundaries. He refers to people who share common values, desires, beliefs, and practices.

Peter was not talking about a nation composed of people who have themselves decided to be part of God's nation. Adoption does not happen because the child decides he wants to be adopted. Adoption is the father's decision, often made before the child is even aware of the possibility. The adopted child is passive in the process, he contributes nothing to the decision. Peter said, "you are a chosen generation" (1 Peter 2:9). Contrary to popular opinion, God does the choosing.

God has chosen His people to bear His glory. God's children will reveal either the glory of salvation (establishing God's great mercy) or the glory of damnation (establishing God's perfect justice). They will demonstrate the fruits of obedience, or the fruits of disobedience. Either way God is glorified. One way reveals the truth of God's mercy, the other the truth of God's justice.

Come!

Jesus Christ is like a sheriff who has a warrant for an outlaw. The sheriff says, "You can either come with me peaceably under your own power because of my kindness, or you can experience the wrath and power of my authority." The outlaw has a choice, but he is going to go with the sheriff either way.

Peter said not only that you (the church) "are a chosen generation, a royal priesthood, an holy nation," but he said that the church is composed of "His own special people (who) proclaim the praises of Him who called you out of darkness into His marvelous light" (1 Peter 2:9). In other words, we are the property of God and He will dispose of us as He chooses. And because we belong to Him and not to ourselves, we cannot complain about His decisions to do with His property as He will.

If a man owns a baseball card collection and decided to save some and burn others he is free to do so. You may disagree with his decision, but you must acknowledge that it is his decision to do what he wants with his own property. So it is with God. But with God the stakes are higher because we are His property!

Here is the point. Take a moment and read Deuteronomy 28:1-24. Don't continue until you do.

Jesus said, "Do not think that I came to destroy the Law or the Prophets. I did not come to destroy but to fulfill" (Matthew 5:17). We live in a critical time in American history. The Rock of Christ is in our path. Will you stumble on the offense of Christ? Or will you claim Jesus Christ as your foundation stone? What will *you* do?

July 7, 1996

The Holy Ghost

These things I have spoken to you, that you should not be made to stumble. They will put you out of the synagogues; yes, the time is coming that whoever kills you will think that he offers God service. And these things they will do to you because they have not known the Father nor Me. But these things I have told you, that when the time comes, you may remember that I told you of them. And these things I did not say to you at the beginning, because I was with you. But now I go away to Him who sent Me, and none of you asks Me, 'Where are You going?' But because I have said these things to you, sorrow has filled your heart. Nevertheless I tell you the truth. It is to your advantage that I go away; for if I do not go away, the Helper will not come to you; but if I depart, I will send Him to you. And when He has come, He will convict the world of sin, and of righteousness, and of judgment: of sin, because they do not believe in Me; of righteousness, because I go to My Father and you see Me no more; of judgment, because the ruler of this world is judged. I still have many things to say to you, but you cannot bear them now. —John 16:1-12

Jesus began here with a reference to "these things." What things? Note first that He mentions *things*—plural. He means to indicate the things that He had been talking about since John 13:31—the new commandment and its implications. Turn in your Bible and look at the headings from John 13:31 forward—The Way, The Truth, And The Life; The Father Revealed, Answered Prayer, The Promise Of Another Helper, The Indwelling Of The Father And Son, The True Vine, The

Perfection Of Love And Joy, And The World's Hatred And Rejection Of The Faithful.

"These things," said Jesus, "I have spoken to you, that you should not be made to stumble" (John 16:1). Knowledge of the things of Christ will keep us from falling under the influence of Satan. The things of Christ will keep us on a straight path. "But," Jesus continued in verse 6, "because I have said these things to you, sorrow has filled your heart."

Not Welcome

Jesus told the faithful back in verse 2 that they would not be welcome in the churches (synagogues) that had accommodated themselves to the world. Faithful Christians would be driven out of churches that did not hold to the gospel. The Jewish synagogues in Jesus' time were of this type, but there is much application to this verse yet today. Churches that do not hold to the gospel cannot tolerate the proclamation of the gospel. Churches that are not led by the Holy Spirit cannot tolerate the leadership of the Holy Spirit. But why not?

"Because it (the world which cannot receive the Spirit of truth) neither sees Him nor knows Him" (John 14:17). The Spirit of truth, the Holy Spirit, is foreign to the world, the Holy Spirit is denied by the world. The world and the Spirit are engaged in a struggle against one another for the souls of men. The spirit of the world and the Spirit of truth cannot coexist in the same human heart. They are mutually exclusive. One must logically overcome the other.

And so what Jesus has said about Himself and the gospel fills worldly hearts with sorrow (see John 16:6). This is, in fact, part of the work of the Holy Spirit—to bring sorrow to worldly hearts, to make them sad because they do not have the Spirit of truth. Jesus does not satisfy the desires (or felt needs) of worldly hearts. Rather, Jesus replaces worldly hearts with kingdom hearts. He replaces worldly desires with kingdom desires, worldly values with godly values. This is the work of the Holy Spirit. This is what being born again is all about—new heart, new life, new desires, new values.

In order to bring His people into willing submission to His special heart transplant surgery, Jesus tells us how He will bring about the change of heart known as conversion. He is like the surgeon who describes to his patients what will happen to them during surgery in order to put them at ease as they face the crisis of surgery.

Imagine your response to a doctor who doesn't tell you in advance what he intends to do. Without understanding the purpose and procedure of surgery, the process would be intolerable. Would you let someone cut you open and rearrange your insides if you did not know his purpose? I wouldn't! And you shouldn't.

So Jesus tells His people the purpose and process He has in mind for their salvation. He is going to give His people new hearts, new desires, new values, new lives, new friendships. Part of the process will come as a new sensitivity of the heart, a sensitivity that will bring with it godly sorrow, which will in turn bring repentance. There will be some pain, but the pain will soon turn to unimaginable joy.

Come Again

Jesus Himself will depart and go to the Father in order to demonstrate His authority. He has submitted Himself to God's authority and judgment, and by God's decree of Christ's righteousness Jesus will direct the Holy Spirit to lead His people in all truth. The righteousness has been granted to Jesus Christ and He has sent the Holy Spirit to come upon His people, to instruct them in the ways of righteousness, and to comfort their sorrow.

"And when He has come," Jesus said (John 16:8), He will do three things. 1) He will convict (or convince) the world of sin, He will convict (or convince) the world of righteousness, and 3) He will convict (or convince) the world by judgment.

The word is *reprove* in the KJV. He will "reprove the world of sin," reprove the world of righteousness and judgment. He will prove again (re-prove) to the world that He was right about sin, right about righteousness and right about judgment. But the light that reveals the truth of God also reveals the falsehood of what is not truth. It is encouraging to understand what is true, but it is disconcerting to be proven wrong. If you have never been proven wrong about your own spiritual beliefs, you have yet to confront the truth of Christ. The identification of what is right also identifies what is wrong.

The Spirit will do three things. First, He will convict the world of sin. This is the first step of the work of the Holy Spirit. Have you ever been convicted of sin? It is not a pleasant experience. It fills the worldly heart with distress and sorrow. The old heart of sin does not want to be replaced. The old heart has grown comfortable with the ways of the world. It enjoys its sins. It likes salt and fat and cheese doodads. It relishes the taste of high cholesterol foods. The cravings of the worldly heart are satisfied by the tastes of a worldly appetite.

Conviction Of Sin

The first action of the Holy Spirit is to reveal the corrupt nature of the cravings of a worldly heart. Those who come under the power of the Holy Spirit are first convinced of the sinfulness of their own appetites and behavior. The very things that people have genuinely enjoyed in the flesh are revealed to be sinful in the Spirit.

But the Spirit is not arguing for the practice of asceticism. The mere avoidance of desires is not godly in itself. There is nothing to be gained by the avoidance of desire.

Rather, desires must be submitted to the authority and leadership of the Holy Spirit. The problem with desires is that they tend to take control of our lives. We easily find ourselves at the mercy of our desires rather than in control of them. In fact, Scripture testifies that we cannot control them. That is why they must be submitted to the Lord. Unless God is the Lord of our lives, we are dominated by the passions of human desire.

We often convince ourselves that we need the things we desire and so we call them needs. We even organize our lives around them to the point that they become the center of much activity—so much so that we find ourselves habitually addicted to them. Sometimes our addictions become so ingrained that we begin to think of them as unalterable personality traits.

Then when the Lord is critical of the things we enjoy, we think that He contradicts Himself because He does not allow for the things He caused us to do because He made us the way we are. When in fact we are behaving in ways that are contrary to the way that He made us, because we have fallen into sin and tarnished His image within us. Then God's call fills our worldly hearts with sorrow—a mental and emotional suffering caused, not by God's criticism of our lifestyle, but by our lack of proper relationship with Him. God doesn't cause it, He just points it out.

The first purpose of the Holy Spirit is to fill us with sorrow for our lack of proper relationship with God. We often misunderstand this godly sorrow, overlooking its necessity and accuse the Spirit of disturbing the peace, when we have mistaken worldly complacency with the peace of God. But God's faithful people must remember that the first purpose and function of the Holy Spirit is to precipitate a personal crisis, to crack the defenses of our worldly values, which we so carefully protect.

Conviction Of Righteousness

The second step (purpose or function) of the Holy Spirit is to reprove the world "of righteousness" (John 16:9). Because there is no righteousness but God's righteousness, and no person in the world is or ever has been righteous but Christ, the righteousness the Spirit endeavors to convince the world of Christ's righteousness. There can be no human righteousness except in and through Christ, and that only through justification by faith in Christ.

The Spirit's second task is to convince sinners that there is no hope for them to ever be acceptable before God, except inasmuch as they have Christ's righteousness given to them by an act of God. We cannot earn Christ's righteousness. God can only give it as a gift. And God only gives it to those who are in Christ by faith. Being in Christ by faith does not mean that what we do is righteous before God, but only that God overlooks what we do because of what Christ has done for us.

The blood of Christ has grafted the faithful into God's tree of righteousness, not that the faithful are thereby capable of righteous behavior by themselves—not at all. But rather, so that the faithful may live.

On the day of judgment everything will be cut down except the tree of God's righteousness. The fruit of God's righteousness is the harvest crop that is to be gathered into God's barn. Everything else will be burned. Only the righteous will inherit the earth beyond the day of judgment.

But there are no righteous people, except in Christ! This is the good news of the gospel. First, the context: judgment is coming. Then the good news: in Christ there is salvation, but only in Christ.

Conviction Of Judgment

However, the approaching judgment is not good news to sinners unless they turn to Christ and believe. Without salvation in Christ, the gospel is a judgment of wrath and eternal damnation. And this is the offense of the gospel. Those who refuse Christ for any reason hear and receive only God's wrath. And that is not good news!

Communication of the whole gospel message is the purpose and function of the Holy Spirit. Those who are not born again rant and rail against God because God doesn't seem fair to them. But those who are born again give thanks and praise God precisely because He is not fair, because they will not receive what in all fairness is coming to them—damnation for their sin.

They are saved by the grace of God who interceded against the fairness of His own judgment. God's righteous anger and judgment against sin is averted by the blood of Christ for those in Christ—those who will believe, who will repent, who will receive the grace and mercy of Christ.

July 14, 1996

Regeneration

This I say, therefore, and testify in the Lord, that you should no longer walk as the rest of the Gentiles walk, in the futility of their mind, having their understanding darkened, being alienated from the life of God, because of the ignorance that is in them, because of the blindness of their heart; who, being past feeling, have given themselves over to lewdness, to work all uncleanness with greediness. But you have not so learned Christ, if indeed you have heard Him and have been taught by Him, as the truth is in Jesus: that you put off, concerning your former conduct, the old man which grows corrupt according to the deceitful lusts, and be renewed in the spirit of your mind, and that you put on the new man which was created according to God, in true righteousness and holiness.

—Ephesians 4:17-24

All Christians are born again. It is not possible to be a Christian and not be born again (John 3:3). It is possible to think that you are born again, but not be (Matthew 7:21). All who are born again necessarily manifest the fruits of righteousness (Matthew 3:8). It is impossible to be born again and not to know it (Acts 3:19). Born again Christians show it (their born-again-ness) in all they do.

Paul described the born again Christian as one who "no longer walks as the rest of the Gentiles walk" (v. 17). That means first of all that born again Christians used to be like Gentiles. Every Christian used to not be a Christian, even those who, like Timothy, were raised as Christians and never knew anything else. This is only to say that every

Christian is familiar with sin. This is a pivotal point of the gospel. Every Christian personally knows his or her own sin. All born again Christians used to be like the Gentiles—used to be, but are no longer like them. Christians are growing into the likeness of Jesus Christ.

To understand this difference we must first understand who and what Gentiles are. Gentiles serve as a kind of reference point in order to mark the change that happens to born again Christians. So, what is a Gentile?

To the Jew a Gentile is anyone who is not Jewish. The Jew believed himself to be faithful to the only true God. So, the real understanding of Gentile is anyone who is not faithful to the only true God.

With the advent of Christ, salvation was opened up to non-Jews. That is the purpose of Christ's ministry—to open up the possibilities of salvation to those who were not born to Jewish parents, and to clarify the gospel for the Jews.

Gentiles were grafted into God's covenant of grace. But Gentiles can no more be born into faithfulness than Jews can. Faithfulness was never a matter of birthright, but always a matter of righteousness before God, which in turn produces the fruit of righteousness—right belief and right conduct.

Misunderstand

Here we are presented with a grand opportunity to misunderstand the gospel. Jesus brought God's covenant of grace to all of the peoples of the world. However, the meaning of that covenant is not that God loves everyone just as they are—unconditionally. (The roots of the idea of unconditional love are in modern psychology, not the Bible.) Rather, the covenant of grace, like all covenants, is a conditional agreement between God and the people of the earth.

The Covenant was offered on the condition of perfect obedience (see Deuteronomy 28). Jesus didn't change the Old Testament covenant, but fulfilled it. Anything less than perfect obedience would bring the wrath of God. And, because no one is perfect or righteous before God, all are under God's wrath. The situation in which all people are born is the inherent inability to meet God's demands for perfection, which means that all people are born to suffer God's wrath. That is our situation, our context.

The covenant of grace can only be satisfied by Jesus Christ because only Christ is righteous. Christ opens up an opportunity to receive God's mercy to all who will believe in Christ, where 'believe in Christ' results in repentance and conversion. To be faithful means to submit to God's will, to agree with God about human sinfulness—and our own personal sinfulness—and God's remedy in Christ, to believe and obey Christ.

Because we human beings are completely unable to satisfy God's demands for perfection, because we are completely unable to be righteous or good in and of ourselves, we cannot save ourselves. Our salvation cannot be accomplished by anything we do. Only God can bring it about. And God has chosen the gospel of Jesus Christ through which to do that.

Change

But God requires a change of mind, a change of heart, a change of behavior. That change is called being born again (John 3:3), or receiving a new heart and new spirit (Ezekiel 11:19; and 36:26), or repentance and conversion (Acts 3:19), or being alive from the dead (Romans 6:13), or being a new creature (2 Corinthians 5:17), or being quickened (Ephesians 2:1), or putting off the old man and putting on the new (Colossians 3:9-10), or washing of regeneration (Titus 3:5), or called out of darkness into light and made a partaker of the divine nature (1 Peter 2:9; and 2 Peter 1:4), or passing from death to life (1 John 3:14). All of these ideas express the same central reality of regeneration, the change of character that is related to salvation. You may come just as you are, but you may not remain just as you are.

Human sinfulness, the willful obstinacy of the human heart has twisted the meaning of God's love. Unregenerate people have perverted God's mercy—offered freely to all sinners—into a kind of blind acceptance of sin on God's part. Sinful people believe that because God is willing to receive them just as they are, that God intends to leave them just as they are. So, rather than repentance they find themselves celebrating their sinfulness—in the name of God or of Jesus Christ!

It is true that God receives people and loves people just as they are, but it is only half the truth. God is willing to receive anyone by the blood of Christ because all sin and all sinners are equal in God's eyes. All recruits are received equally into God's boot camp. God's mercy is not the end of salvation, but the beginning. God demands a great change of character—so much so that there is no salvation for those who do not demonstrate the fruits of such a change.

The change of heart that God requires cannot be counterfeited. You and I are not always able to identify a born again Christian, but God can. Every truly born again Christian produces the fruit of regeneration, but only God can discern the actual condition of the heart. So, the best that we can do for one another is to help each other identify and manifest the fruits of regeneration.

Evidence

The church must insist on the evidence of a changed heart and a changed life in all of her members. To do less is to invite corruption into the church, and to be disobedient ourselves. Consequently, we must ask, what are the evidences of a changed heart? Paul answers this concern negatively in verse 17. Born again Christians should not live like the unfaithful—lying, cheating, being selfish, and the like. Regenerate Christians should not covet the things of the world.

Their walk should be distinguishable from the walk of the unfaithful. Such a walk will certainly require modesty of dress, humility of attitude, and meekness of behavior. Humble people do not strut their stuff. Meek people do not dress in the flag of rebellion. Loving people do not argue with God-given authorities—parents, elders, or governmental authorities (teachers or tax collectors). Born again parents do not allow their children to be exposed to the influences of lust and disobedience.

The children of born again Christians are not free to do what they want. They are not free to watch what they want to watch. They are not free to go where they want to go, or to choose their own friends. They are not free because God has given their parents the responsibility to expose them to what is Godly in the hope of their salvation. Born again parents are responsible to teach the faith to their own children, to keep their children from the temptations of the world in the hope of their salvation, as best they can. Christians are under authority, and so are their children.

Christians are to be in the world but not of the world. But people twist this truth into an excuse to indulge themselves in worldliness. God has nothing against wealth or technology. We should all know that. Wealth is a great gift, and technology is its fruit. The issue is not how much you have, but what you are doing with what you have. God asks, "who is the primary beneficiary of your wealth?" Are you serving your own interests? Or are you serving God's interests?

The issue is regeneration, not wealth. Anyone can be wealthy, with a little work. Anyone can participate in the tax benefits of nonprofit contributions. Anyone can contribute to causes that will bring favorable social standing. But only regenerate Christians, who stand on the integrity of God's Word, give generously to God's cause. God set the minimum support at ten percent. Ten percent is not a goal to be striven for, it is the minimum standard from which to begin. The greater your wealth, the greater God's expectation of you.

A true testimony of faithfulness is found in our checkbook registers. There one's real values are clearly and easily discerned. So, take your checkbook into prayer and examine your faithfulness with God's measure.

Paul shows us positively what we should be and do, and negatively what we should not be and not do. By implication Paul identified the marks of a Gentile—futility of the mind, darkened understanding, alienation from God, ignorance of God's Word, blindness of the heart, no sensitivity to God, lewdness (not only foul mouthed and lustful, but rude and unmannerly), uncleanness, dishonesty, and greediness. These are the fruits of unregeneracy, fruits of the degenerate.

Born Again

Regeneration by the holy Spirit is all God's doing. If you are born again it is of no credit to yourself. You cannot do it to yourself. Nor is it the result of what or who you are. Yet, Scripture is clear that, even though you cannot accomplish it, if you are not born again it is entirely your own fault. Even though we cannot accomplish regeneration, we are all responsible to put ourselves in God's way. We must make ourselves available to the movement of the Spirit. We (the church) must prepare ourselves to receive the Spirit, though that preparation will contribute nothing to our salvation.

If you are not born again it is entirely your own fault! Why? Because God "so loved the world that He gave His only begotten Son, that whoever believes in Him should not perish but have everlasting life" (John 3:16). Whoever believes! God does not withhold salvation from anyone, but commands all. Whoever believes is welcome. But we must realize that God is serious about the change of heart that He requires. Whoever believes must also be changed.

Notice that God begins with the mind, "be renewed in the spirit of your mind" (v. 24). God begins with belief because our beliefs give direction to our conscience, and our conscience guides our behavior. Godly behavior will result from a rightly informed conscience, and ungodly behavior from a poorly formed conscience, regardless of one's election status.

When we try to address the behavior of others directly, we become tyrants and dictators, imposing our will on others. Have you ever noticed that when you try to correct the behavior of your children they struggle against you? They struggle against you because they know that they have been created free. So when authorities (parents, elders, governments) try to correct behavior, they limit human freedom. People struggle against that. Such an approach quickly becomes legalistic and authoritarian.

In contrast to this, God seeks to correct our beliefs. By correcting our beliefs God both informs our conscience and allows for our freedom. A Christian conscience will produce Christian behavior—freely, willingly. A person with a Christian conscience will freely choose to behave like a Christian.

God's primary emphasis is on belief, not behavior. As God's people, as God's instruments in the world, our primary emphasis must also be on belief. A correct understanding of God will produce a God-informed conscience. Then, by the power of the Holy Spirit, godly behavior will be the free choice of a God-informed conscience, either out of love and gratitude for God's grace or out of fear and loathing of God's justice.

Consequently, God calls His people to theological clarity, not simply moral instruction. The first fruit of regeneration is a renewed interest in God's Word, where theology is the study of God and His Word, the Bible. Those who are born again find new interest in Bible study. A passion for Bible study is the first mark of a born again Christian.

July 21, 1996

Perseverance

Grace to you and peace from God our Father and the Lord Jesus Christ. I thank my God, making mention of you always in my prayers, hearing of your love and faith which you have toward the Lord Jesus and toward all the saints, that the sharing of your faith may become effective by the acknowledgment of every good thing which is in you in Christ Jesus. For we have great joy and consolation in your love, because the hearts of the saints have been refreshed by you, brother. Therefore, though I might be very bold in Christ to command you what is fitting, yet for love's sake I rather appeal to you—being such a one as Paul, the aged, and now also a prisoner of Jesus Christ—I appeal to you for my son Onesimus, whom I have begotten while in my chains, who once was unprofitable to you, but now is profitable to you and to me. —*Philemon 1:3-11*

Paul persevered in faithfulness because he remembered the Philippians "always in every prayer...making request for (them) with all joy" (v. 3). To persevere in the faith is to remember.

Remembering is an action—literally to reconnect, or to member again, where the word *member* is used as a verb. A member (noun) is a part of something larger. So, to use member as a verb is to suggest an activity that contributes toward one's membership in something larger. In the case of the church perseverance means to perform your membership function as a part of Christ's body. It means to utilize your spiritual gift. It means to be available to the will of God.

To persevere is to be persistent regarding one's church membership, to stubbornly practice church membership in the face of the many things that tend to pull us away from the Lord. To persevere is to say "yes" to church and "no" to the boat, to say "yes" to Sunday School and "no" to soccer, "yes" to Bible study and "no" to television. I don't mean that you should never go boating, or never play soccer, or never watch television. But when there is a conflict between them the person who perseveres in the faith says "yes" to the things of the faith.

I also don't mean that perfect church attendance is required. Don't be absurd. Things come up. Things happen. The church is not the only institution in America. However, I do mean consistent and persistent attention to Christ and His church. While missing worship once in a while is not a sign of negligence, it should be observed that backsliding begins with little things and easy excuses.

Perseverance in itself is not a virtue. To persevere in sin, to persevere in lust, gluttony, or greed, is not what Paul had in mind here. Perseverance in itself is neither good nor bad. It is the object of perseverance that makes the difference. The end or the principle that guides our perseverance is important. Paul had in mind persevering toward the right end—Christ's purpose.

Stubborn

Another word for perseverance is *stubbornness.* Stubbornness in itself is neither good nor bad. It depends on what you are stubborn about. To be stubborn for Christ and the things of Christ is good. But to be stubborn in our own desires is not. To stubbornly cling to the truth of the Bible is a virtue. But to stubbornly cling to your own opinion is a well-worn path to death and destruction.

The mule is the state animal of Missouri. You may have heard that Missourians are famous for their stubbornness. A story I heard related to the stubbornness of mule-minded Missourians. It's a story about the difference between horses and mules. Apparently, when a herd of horses is attacked by a pack of wolves, if the horses can't outrun them, they will form a circle with their heads to the center and kick like the devil with their hind legs, setting up a defensive wall of flying hooves.

A mule is the offspring of a horse and an donkey. Apparently, mules never got the right defensive gene. Mules are half-breeds. More correctly, says the dictionary, a mule is the "offspring of a jackass and a mare, as distinguished from a hinny."

Anyway, when mules are attacked by wolves, they also form a circle. But instead of putting their heads in the center of the circle, they keep their heads to the outside of the circle, and kick like the devil. The bottom line is that the mules end up hurting each other as the wolves sit back and watch the show.

It's a story about persevering in the church. Mules are stubborn, but they are not team players. The kind of perseverance that Paul was talking about is the perseverance of a team player. It is the perseverance of remembering God and of being a member of Christ's body.

It is all too common to confuse the act of stubbornly clinging to one's own opinion with faithful perseverance. Sure, there are times when God's people are called to stand alone against the world. Faithful Christians need to be prepared for those times, ready to stand alone when so called.

Not Alone

But generally the church is not the place to stand alone. The church is not the place to celebrate the differing opinions of her members. Rather, the church is the place to celebrate God's opinion, given in His Word, and the unity of agreement about God's opinion. God isn't so concerned about our various opinions about this and that. Rather, God is concerned that we agree with His opinion regarding sin and salvation. Our persistence must match God's persistence. We must be persistent in the same ways and toward the same ends as God is. When our methods or purposes differ from God's we stand in opposition to God.

The ancient Israelites had to persist in following God in the wilderness. They moved when God moved, by pillar of smoke by day and by pillar of fire by night. And they didn't move when God didn't move. To move when God doesn't move, or not to move when He does, is to persist in the wrong thing.

We need to be firm where Christ is firm, and to be flexible where Christ is flexible. The church is not about doing our own thing. It is about doing God's thing. In fact, this matter of perseverance is not really about our perseverance at all. It's about God's perseverance. God determines the methods of perseverance. God determines the ends of perseverance. God determines the people to persevere. We can persevere for God only because Christ persevered for us.

Paul said it this way, "He who has begun a good work in you will complete it" (v. 6). God will finish what He began. The perseverance of God's faithful people is God's desire and God's doing. And whatever God desires happens. But it happens in God's time and by God's methods.

Paul was a stubborn preacher. Nothing would stop him from preaching Christ crucified and risen. He had been shipwrecked, beaten, imprisoned, run out of town—yet he persisted. His perseverance was not a matter of his own choosing. He did not persevere in his own opinion. God changed his mind. He did not persevere in his old ways of doing things. God changed his mind and his habits.

Paul's perseverance was grounded in God's love. God had chosen him. God loved him first. Without God's initiative Paul would not have loved God, not really. Paul's love of God grew over the years. It wasn't there at first. Paul was blinded by God when he was on his way to persecute Christians. Paul didn't decide to get saved. God blinded him and threw him in the dust. But because God chose him and persevered in loving and protecting him, Paul came to love the Lord over time.

Had any of it depended upon Paul's ability to persevere in loving God, it would have come to nothing. But because God persevered, Paul was saved. And what is true of Paul is true of us. God loves us, and will persevere in loving us. But that doesn't mean that we will escape life's difficulties—shipwreck, beatings, prison, being run out of town, sickness, pain, disease, whatever.

Perseverance is not about our ability to hang in there with God. It is about God's willingness to hang in there with us. Because Christ perseveres with us, we can persevere in Him.

God sent Jesus to persevere on our behalf. The Lord has done His part. Have you done yours?

July 28, 1996

Resurrection of Damnation

There was a certain rich man who was clothed in purple and fine linen and fared sumptuously every day. But there was a certain beggar named Lazarus, full of sores, who was laid at his gate, desiring to be fed with the crumbs which fell from the rich man's table. Moreover the dogs came and licked his sores. So it was that the beggar died, and was carried by the angels to Abraham's bosom. The rich man also died and was buried. And being in torments in Hades, he lifted up his eyes and saw Abraham afar off, and Lazarus in his bosom. Then he cried and said, "Father Abraham, have mercy on me, and send Lazarus that he may dip the tip of his finger in water and cool my tongue; for I am tormented in this flame." But Abraham said, "Son, remember that in your lifetime you received your good things, and likewise Lazarus evil things; but now he is comforted and you are tormented. And besides all this, between us and you there is a great gulf fixed, so that those who want to pass from here to you cannot, nor can those from there pass to us." Then he said, "I beg you therefore, father, that you would send him to my father's house, for I have five brothers, that he may testify to them, lest they also come to this place of torment." Abraham said to him, "They have Moses and the prophets; let them hear them." And he said, "No, father Abraham; but if one goes to them from the dead, they will repent." But he said to him, "If they do not hear Moses and the prophets, neither will they be persuaded though one rise from the dead." —*Luke 16:19-31*

A Japanese visitor to an American small town asked the tour guide why there were two churches across the street from each other. "Isn't one enough?" he asked. The tour guide thought for a moment and the remarked, "The church on the north side says there is no hell, but the church on the south corner says, 'The hell there isn't!"

Heaven and hell, what are we to make of them in our day? The possibilities for speculation are endless. Rivers of ink have been poured out in the effort to make sense of them. Dante's Medieval classic, *The Divine Comedy*, set the standard for belief about heaven and hell. While Dante's intention may have been to write a political parody of his day, what is remembered is not his politics, but this three-tiered description of reality—heaven above, hell below, and earth in the middle.

This three-tiered reality, more the work of Dante's imagination than an honest description of the biblical truth, continues to haunt the modern imagination. People today still think in terms of heaven above and hell below, even though modern physics has made every effort to refute such a childish understanding.

How are we to think of heaven and hell? Are they real? Or are they just literary devices used to motivate people to a particular behavior? Are heaven and hell actual places? Or what?

The Old Testament word *sheol* is often translated as hell. Sheol was an actual place. It was the place of refuse. It was the refuse pit, the garbage dump of Israel—outside their main camping area and later outside the walls of Jerusalem. Because it was often a pit, it implied down or below. Sheol was also used as an analogy for the eternal place of refuse for unsaved souls.

The New Testament uses two words for hell, *hades* and *geenna*. *Hades* was used to indicate a spiritual realm of perdition. The "term came to denote the place of temporary sojourn prior to resurrection (c.f. Isaiah 26:19)."[3]

Hell is the place of the future punishment. This was originally the valley of Hinnom, south of Jerusalem, where the filth and dead animals of the city were cast out and burned. It was a fit symbol of the wicked and their future destruction.

The great danger when discussing heaven and hell is to launch out into human speculation, to use the Bible as a jumping off place, to try to fit our speculations into biblical terminology. But it must be remembered that what is important is not what you and I think of heaven and hell, but what God's Word tells us of them. What the Bible says can be

3 *Theological dictionary of the New Testament.*, by Geoffrey W. Bromily, p. 22.

trusted, and what it doesn't say must be left alone.

The Bible continually warns us not to rely upon our imaginations, but to trust in God's Word only. Human imagination quickly leads into fantasy and error. But with that warning firmly in mind, let me say a few things about heaven from a modern perspective.

It is interesting to realize that heaven has traditionally been understood to be an abode that lies above the earth. Not much more is said about its location in Scripture, but that much has been revealed. We know that Jesus was with the Father in heaven when the world was created. And we know that he ascended into heaven in the air or in the clouds some forty days after His resurrection. Heaven is described as an abode above the earth. We also know that God predestined the elect to live with Him in heaven for all eternity.

Now add to this store of information the modern reality of space exploration and the fact that a space station is presently under construction, and you have a very interesting situation. Not a fantasy, but a reality.

If God knew everything from the beginning, then God knew that eventually we would build a space station. We don't know yet whether such an enterprise will prove viable or futile, but it is not a function of human fantasy. It is a present reality. The practical implications of this modern reality related to the biblical concept of heaven are yet to be developed. Consequently, it is certainly interesting ground for reflection.

If the heavenly abode has such a present reality, what about the reality of hell? Can we apply the idea of a refuse pit or garbage dump existence to the modern world? You bet we can. When we look at the vast amounts of pollution and garbage generated by modern society, we come face to face with another potential reality from which there may be no recovery. Such a thought may point toward an eternal hell.

However, it must be noted that the biblical concepts of heaven and hell are set in eternity, not in time. Heaven and hell are eternal abodes relating to an "afterlife." Here is where the analogies fall short. Human understanding cannot embrace eternity. That is, eternity is a greater period of time than human beings are able to comprehend.

Time

But because heaven and hell are understood biblically in terms of eternity, perhaps we can better conceive of them in terms of time, rather than place (or space). Much of God's salvation plan is presented in temporal terminology. The time was *ripe* for Jesus to come. The time for salvation is *now*. No one knows the time of the Day of the Lord.

Consequently, heaven and hell may be better understood in categories of time and history, rather than as actual places, above or below.

Because they are eternal, heaven and hell may be better represented by time language than place language. Perhaps heaven and hell are very long historical time periods, during which the activities of heaven and hell occur. Certainly, the leading edge of God's kingdom (or heaven) has broken into human history with the advent of Jesus Christ.

Are we getting too carried away with human speculation? Or are we more closely approaching a description that is more fundamentally biblical in nature? Are we being more realistic or more imaginative? Sometimes it is hard to tell. But when in doubt, cling to Scripture.

Rich Man

Jesus told three stories of "a certain rich man." Each time the story had a moral for the rich man, and each moral was essentially the same: Don't squander your time and money on the things of this world. The first two stories are about this world, the last is about the next world. The first story is called The Parable of the Rich Fool (Luke 12:16-21), the second, The Parable of the Unjust Steward, (Luke 16:1-13), and the third, The Rich Man and Lazarus (Luke 16:19-31).

The rich man was never named, but Lazarus was. Lazarus was not a rich man, but a poor man. The rich man was selfish and greedy, Lazarus was not. Nor was Lazarus pining his time away coveting what the rich man had. Lazarus was not hoping or trying to strike it rich. Rather, Lazarus was content with his poverty. We know this because Lazarus desired to be fed with only the crumbs from his master's table.

He didn't want what the master had, but would have been happy with crumbs. He was not a threat to the rich man's wealth, even had the rich man wanted to help poor Lazarus. Lazarus would have been an easy person to help because he would have been satisfied with very little.

Lazarus lay at the rich man's gate. He was a poor beggar seeking alms from this "certain rich man." But because dogs came and licked poor Lazarus' sores we can infer that he received no help. The rich man passed him by without so much as a kind word.

Lazarus died "and was carried by the angels to Abraham's bosom" (v. 22). And the rich man also died "and was buried" (v. 23). We can assume that Abraham's bosom was up and that burial was down. The one went to heaven and the other to hell. It is interesting to note that Calvin thought this story to have been an actual historical event, rather than a mere parable with a punch.

We often assume that the rich man was thirsty in hell, but Scripture doesn't really say that. The verse speaks of his tongue suffering the torment of hell fire. When we get hot, we get thirsty, and perhaps that's all it means. But it should be noted that the focus of the rich man's torment was his tongue, not his thirst.

James said that "the tongue is a fire, a world of iniquity. The tongue is so set among our members that it defiles the whole body, and sets on fire the course of nature; and it is set on fire by hell" (James 3:6).

Jesus never said exactly what this rich man's sins were. We can infer greed and selfishness, but we also know that sins tend to cluster together. Where one is, there are many. It may be hot in hell, and people may get thirsty there. But have you ever burned your tongue? It's a bummer.

Communication

Another observation we can make from Jesus' description of heaven and hell here is that there is communication between them, but not travel. The rich man and Lazarus could see one another—at least the rich man could see Lazarus. But he never talked to him. He only conversed with Abraham, who served as a type or analogy for Christ. I imagine it was like a closed window or a video camera without sound.

There was a "great gulf fixed" between them, which eliminated the possibility of travel. It also appears that all communication was mediated by Abraham (or Christ—God really). There were a few occasions of travel between heaven and earth. "Elijah went up by a whirlwind into heaven" (2 Kings 2:11); He also called fire down from heaven (2 Kings 1:10); Jesus was seen on the Mount of Transfiguration with Moses and Elijah; and Jesus "was taken up, and a cloud received Him out of their sight" (Acts 1:9); and a few other incidents involving transportation between heaven and earth, and hell and earth. But never do we find any transportation directly between heaven and hell, although Abraham (Christ or God) is able to communicate with both realms.

The moral of this story is, of course, that there is a time beyond which salvation is no longer possible. It is possible while people live on this earth, but not beyond. This life provides a one-way ticket to heaven or hell.

Reward

We don't know much about the nature of heaven or hell, and we are probably not supposed to. All we really know is that one is a place or time of reward, and the other a place or time of punishment. And the deciding factor is not how we live our lives on earth, although that may play an important part in the determination of our destination. Works are important! But the deciding factor is Jesus Christ.

Jesus can redeem poor sinners and punish the righteous rich. Our future destination is in His hands. And His judgments are beyond our ability to lobby for a particular decision.

The point is that heaven and hell are real. Judgment is real. There is no getting out of it. But when people convince themselves that heaven and hell are not real, they can then also perceive no need for Jesus. If salvation is real, if Jesus is really who He says He is, then heaven and hell are also real. You can't be a Christian and believe in salvation unless you believe heaven and hell are real.

Christians who don't believe in the reality of heaven or hell are fooling themselves.

August 11, 1996

The Resurrection of Salvation

But I do not want you to be ignorant, brethren, concerning those who have fallen asleep, lest you sorrow as others who have no hope. For if we believe that Jesus died and rose again, even so God will bring with Him those who sleep in Jesus. For this we say to you by the word of the Lord, that we who are alive and remain until the coming of the Lord will by no means precede those who are asleep. For the Lord Himself will descend from heaven with a shout, with the voice of an archangel, and with the trumpet of God. And the dead in Christ will rise first. Then we who are alive and remain shall be caught up together with them in the clouds to meet the Lord in the air. And thus we shall always be with the Lord. Therefore comfort one another with these words. —*1 Thessalonians 4:13-18*

Brother, are you saved?" The first time I heard the question I didn't like it because it implied that I might not be saved. I rationalized that God is love, and God loves people, therefore God will save everyone. What kind of God would not save everyone? I convinced myself that I wanted nothing to do with a God who would not save everyone.

I had been groomed for such a decision by the kind of preaching I had heard all my life. Many preachers believe, or at least preach, only the "God is love" stuff of the Bible. Such was the liberality of my home church tradition.

"Sister, are you saved?" What kind of question is that, anyway? In order to answer it, you must know what salvation is, what you are saved from and what you are saved for. Can you define salvation? If you can't, you probably aren't.

Traditionally, salvation is understood to be the work of God in three acts. Act one is justification, act two—sanctification, and act three—glorification. Let me briefly define these terms and then come back to them in Scripture and draw out the implications and applications of the text.

Justification

Justification is commonly associated with grace because it is entirely the decision and action of God to provide the righteousness necessary to receive people into His presence. Because God is holy, He cannot tolerate sin. Therefore, He cannot tolerate sinners in His presence. Consequently, their sin must be dealt with first.

Sin is destroyed by the light of God. So, when a sinner comes into the presence of God he is destroyed because he identifies himself with his sin. The fact that all people are sinners made God very lonely with regard to people; and because God is love, and because love requires interaction with other people, God cannot tolerate loneliness because love requires others to love.

But neither can God be unjust, so He cannot tolerate sin.

So, there God is: loving but just—and lonely because all people are sinners. Sinners cannot have fellowship with God because they are destroyed as they draw near to God's presence. What to do?

God devised a plan whereby sinners who willingly stand under the lordship of His Son, Jesus Christ, can thereby freely receive Christ's righteousness. And by receiving Christ's righteousness they can draw near to God for fellowship, and God can be both loving and just. God's demands for righteousness would be met by granting the righteousness of Christ to those who believe.

God knew that Christ would complete His mission of making His people righteous over time. God's trust of Christ's ability to accomplish His plan allowed God to make a decree of righteousness granted to all who would freely claim Christ as Lord and Savior. The purpose of this great plan was to allow the likes of you and me to grow in righteousness (even unto perfection), while at the same time preserving the integrity of God's character, as both loving and just.

The decree of God is called justification, and it is ours, or we are under it when we proclaim belief and obedience in Christ. Justification —God's decree of righteousness given to all who are in Christ—is entirely God's action in the counsels of heaven. Certainly, we must respond to God. But our response in no way causes God to act. God acted before we even arrived on the scene.

We are like condemned criminals on death row, waiting for execution. Suddenly the governor grants us pardon. The pardon is his decision, not ours. We only passively receive it. It is critical that we understand that the receiving of the governor's pardon is not the cause of his decision to grant it. The governor had already decided and acted when we received it.

Justification is God's pardon. Our receiving it is simply a matter of receiving word (or news) of it. "Did you hear that God granted pardon to sinners on death row?" Hearing (or receiving) that news is called justification. It provides a kind of justification for godly joy.

Included in the Governor's pardon is not only a stay of execution, but his promise to work through the courts for the eventual release of the prisoners in return for their good behavior. The Governor's pardon does not get a person out of prison, it only stays the execution. The death sentence has been canceled and the promise of early release for good behavior is then set before the pardoned prisoners.

Sanctification

The good behavior clause in God's pardon is known as sanctification. Sanctification is also known as growth in grace, or spiritual growth. It is part of God's deal, but it requires time to play itself out. Understand that God will not renege on His Word. He will provide a good behavior release to all who behave good. The opportunity is set equally before all, no matter what their sin. The only requirements are accepting the stay of execution and, of course, the good behavior.

God knows that Jesus will accomplish His purpose in all who believe in Him. It's a sure thing, a done deal. It's not a complicated contract, just a pardon, and release for good behavior. God knows that Jesus Christ has the power to complete it because God gave Him the power to do just that.

Justification is God's acceptance of sinners who claim allegiance to Christ, with the understanding that allegiance to Christ will bring eventual righteousness. Sanctification is the growth in grace and righteousness that comes with allegiance to Christ. Sanctification brings improvement in one's morality and behavior. But these are only the preliminaries for fellowship with God.

Glorification

In time the prisoner (sinner) will be released into fellowship with God. That release is called glorification. It is the glorification of God because it is the completion of God's plan. And upon that completion there will be a great celebration. That's glorification.

Fellowship with God in heaven requires righteousness. There is no room for sin (error) in heaven with God. God cannot tolerate sin. The unrighteous are not welcome. They will be destroyed by their sin and unrighteousness if they ever somehow reach heaven. Salvation, then, involves all of these—justification, sanctification, and glorification, and leads to fellowship with God. Salvation is not complete until all of these are complete.

In verse 13 Paul said that he did not want people to be ignorant of all this because such ignorance amounts to death. To be ignorant of something really means to ignore it. Ignoring God's plan is certain death.

Paul writes of death as if it were sleep, or sleep as if it were death. In the margins of your Bible you will see that verse 13 can be translated as either "fallen asleep" or "died." I don't want to make too much of this, but it should be noted that the Greek word is neither *necros*, death, nor *katheudo*, to sleep. The word is *koimao*, which means to lay down to sleep, with the emphasis on the laying down, not the sleeping. Sleep involves laying down and getting up.

Indeed, death is a kind of sleep, and sleep is a kind of death. The thing Paul points to here is that death is not the end, but there will be a waking up after death. That's the point Paul makes. We should make no more, but no less of it than that. Death is only a kind of lying down. It's not the end.

Those who believe in Jesus when they lay down to sleep, still believe in Jesus in the morning when they wake up. So it is in death. The relationship of faithfulness to Christ is not destroyed by death. Those who die in Christ will also rise in Christ, just as those who die without Christ will rise without Christ. Our relationship with God is not changed by death. God's blessings and curses will prevail beyond death.

Many Thessalonians had been faithful all their lives, and into death. Paul simply wanted to assure them that their reward (fellowship with God in heaven) would still be in effect beyond death. Indeed, Paul said, they would be received (or resurrected) first, when Jesus returned.

Paul goes on to specify (to a degree) the details of Christ's return. "The Lord Himself will descend from heaven with a shout" (v. 16). The Greek word for *shout* here means a command or a cry of incitement. To incite is to arouse or to set in motion, to stir up, or spur on. It is a call to action. Christ will come down from heaven above with a call to action.

We might well ask, "A call to what action?" If Christ is going to shout a command we need to know what He wants, or at least to anticipate His intention. We might not be able to know all the specifics of it, but perhaps we can anticipate its general tenor. What action? What command?

Verse 16 is divided into two sentences. The second sentence indicates the action that will follow Christ's command. "The dead in Christ will rise first." The action is rise. Paul goes on, "Then we who are alive and remain shall be caught up together with them in the clouds to meet the Lord in the air" (v. 17). This, of course, is known in the contemporary world as the rapture.

While the word *rapture* does not occur in the Bible, it is implied by this verse. From the Latin, it means to carry away, or to be carried away with. One is raptured when he is carried away with or by Christ. The prepositional difference (*with* or *by*) is crucial. One interpretation suggests emotional enthusiasm, the other may suggest evacuation. Correct me if I'm wrong, but it sounds to me like an emergency evacuation of some sort may have been anticipated by the Lord.

Evacuation

We are again running into the difficulty of knowing the difference between speculation and reality. For most of human history an emergency air support evacuation was mere speculation, but today, particularly with a space station presently under construction, it may fall into the realm of reality. What a thought!

While the notion of an emergency evacuation may be within the universe of discourse of this verse, it is certainly not the entire meaning of the verse. Nor perhaps the most important meaning. We know that because, even if it were true, the preparation for such an event is more time consuming than the event itself. Even if it were true, in our day the preparation would be the main event, as it has been throughout Christian history. And the preparation, more than mere technology, would involve converting the hearts and minds of God's people to believe such a reality.

God's people are always called to respond to the movement of God's Spirit. Emergency evacuation is not a foreign idea in the Bible. Consider Noah, Abraham, Lot—even the forced evacuation of Israel and Jerusalem during their destruction in A.D. 70.

Here & Now

Paul concludes with two thoughts. First, that if we are properly prepared in heart and mind "we shall always be with the Lord" (v. 17). That's the primary thing about faithfulness: we are called, not merely to a future event (life in heaven, or the rapture, or an emergency evacuation, or whatever), but we are primarily called to a present relationship with God through Jesus Christ His Son. We are called to a relationship with Jesus Christ regardless of what else may happen.

We are called primarily to be "with the Lord." Daily, weekly, monthly, yearly, all our lives, in relationship with the Lord. And what is more we are called to bring our children and our grandchildren into relationship with the Lord. In this way we will always be prepared to go with the Lord wherever and whenever He calls.

Paul found great comfort in this description of the return of Christ. And he commends us to find comfort in it as well. The comfort is that, no matter what happens in this world, God has a plan for His people. We can persist in faithfulness because God has a plan. We may not understand it all, but God does. We need only trust God to accomplish it.

But it is not enough to derive comfort from God's Word. Paul also calls us to "comfort one another with these words" (v. 18). First, we must be comforted ourselves. That is to say, we must believe the gospel. But belief is not enough. We must then go out and comfort others, help others to believe. This is not an after thought, but is the very heart of the gospel.

Feed on the Word of God yourself, then, share the food.

August 18, 1996

Christian Unity

I do not pray for these alone, but also for those who will believe in Me through their word; that they all may be one, as You, Father, are in Me, and I in You; that they also may be one in Us, that the world may believe that You sent Me. And the glory which You gave Me I have given them, that they may be one just as We are one: I in them, and You in Me; that they may be made perfect in one, and that the world may know that You have sent Me, and have loved them as You have loved Me. Father, I desire that they also whom You gave Me may be with Me where I am, that they may behold My glory which You have given Me; for You loved Me before the foundation of the world. O righteous Father! The world has not known You, but I have known You; and these have known that You sent Me. And I have declared to them Your name, and will declare it, that the love with which You loved Me may be in them, and I in them. —*John 17:20-26*

This, no doubt, is the most important prayer that Jesus prayed. Christian unity is a central theme of the Bible. But it is not a theme that stands alone. In fact, no Scriptural theme (doctrine) stands alone, but all are interwoven in a tapestry of divine interrelatedness. That is why to seize upon any particular theme or doctrine and consider it without reference to others always leads to error and misunderstanding.

The theme of unity is bolstered by the related themes of regeneration, love, peace, charity, and understanding. And for further clarification it is contrasted against its opposite: separation—not mere diversity, but separation. Just as Christian unity is a chief doctrine, so is Christian separation from worldliness, pride, and the host of accompanying sins. Unity without such separation is shy of the biblical mark, just as separation without unity is also shy of the mark.

Ecumenical

The difficulty in today's ecumenical world is that those who cry for unity have no equal passion for separation, and those who cry for separation (against the ecumenical effort) have no equal passion for Christian unity. The truth is to be found at the point of tension between the opposing concerns for unity and for separation—not the flaccid condition of mere balance, but the vigor of a healthy tension between the unity of the saints and their separation from worldliness.

Jesus begins this prayer by lifting up His concern for the unborn. He prayed not "for these alone," meaning those who already believe, but He also prayed "for those who will believe." Here we see Jesus' concern for His "other sheep" (John 10:16) which He must yet bring. His concern is not simply for those presently alive, but for the future, for those who would be born in the future who would believe in Christ. Certainly, not all the unborn will believe in Christ, but some will—many will, probably even most. And for their sake He prayed the prayer of Christian unity.

In today's world we hear much talk about the desire for Christian unity, but we do not hear the equally important talk about separation from all ungodliness. There is today much concern for the unity of the organized church, a unity between and among denominations. But denominational unity can only be a unity built upon man-made foundations because denominations are themselves man-made.

In contrast, biblical unity can only be built upon the spiritual foundations laid by Jesus Christ. Christian unity can only become a reality when Christians are unified by regeneration in Christ and separate themselves from the sinful influences of the world, and from the worldliness that has crept into the church.

We hear hew and cry for the unity of all people today, yet we kill our own unborn children in numbers that can only compare to the greatest war in history or an incredible natural disaster. We have shut our ears to Jesus' concern for Christian unity with the unborn. And by doing so we disregard His prayer for unity.

Jesus prayed "that (we) may be one" (v. 21). His choice of words suggests that the unity for which He prayed was not a present reality for His people. It wasn't then, nor is it yet. The fullness of the unity that Jesus prayed for has never been a reality, but always a distant hope.

Trinitarian

But neither was the unity that Jesus prayed for to be some kind of superstructure that imposed a man-made conformity upon the churches of Christ. Christ did not conceive His unity to be organizational, but organic, not administrative, but spiritual. Not a superstructure of bishops or para-church organizations, but a spiritual unity of common purpose, common love, common charity, a unity of heart and mind. Not that everyone should think and believe alike, but that all thinking and believing would be grounded in the unified reality of the Trinitarian Godhead, that our diverse thinking and believing would contribute to spiritual growth and worship in truth and in spirit.

Jesus spoke of a unity that mirrored His relationship with the Father—God in Christ, Christ in God, and Christ in His people. Not Methodists and Baptists and Presbyterians and Congregationalists, etc., but Christians in Christ and Christ in Christians.

Jesus continued in verse 22, "that they may be one just as We are one." Just as Christ is one with the Father, we are to be one with one another. Christ and God are one in terms of belief, yet their language at times differs greatly. Christ and God are one in terms of mission, yet there is a world of difference between law and grace. Yet, even in law and grace there is unity in Christ. Not apart from Christ, but in Christ only do law and grace cohere in Christian unity. Only in Christ does the language of the Old Testament reveal its harmony with the language of the New Testament. Only in Christ.

Consequently, Christian unity will be found only in Christ, not in denominations, not in missions, not in inter-church cooperation. Only in Christ. I fear that the contemporary vision of Christian unity is beyond human capacity. Like children at a sumptuous feast, our eyes are bigger than our stomachs! Certainly, the contemporary quest for unity is beyond the vision Christ gave to His disciples.

The contemporary cry for Christian unity is a vision that well-meaning, but over-extended, Christians borrowed from the modern capitalistic, resource-pooling world and applied to the Church. The world teaches that there is strength in numbers, God teaches that there is strength in the weakness that depends upon Christ (2 Corinthians 12:19). The biblical vision of Christian unity is based on a different vision. God's vision for unity is not an organizational merger, but a spiritual coalescence.

Overstep

Biblical unity consists of brothers and sisters cooperating in Christian belief and practice, friends and neighbors united in local mission.

Biblical unity is not a matter of the hierarchical meshing of denominations, but the equality of thinking and believing together as brothers and sisters, friends and neighbors. Modern thinking has overstepped the bounds of biblical unity. No wonder it isn't working! It can't work because it is not God's vision.

The failure of the church today is a direct reflection upon its lack of biblical unity. The purpose of Christian unity is that the world may know and believe that Christ has been sent by God to save the world (John 17:23). So, when the world doesn't believe the gospel, you can look to a lack of Christian unity as the cause. Faithful Christian ministry requires the unity that Christ prayed for—primarily spiritual unity, not simply organizational unity.

To inspire His people toward unity, Christ bestowed glory upon His people. In verse 24 Christ prayed that God allow His people to "be with Me where I am." Why? In order to behold His glory. In order to fully experience the glory of Christ, His people need to be where He is. But where is He? At the time He prayed this prayer He was with His disciples on earth. But now He is in heaven. His intention is not merely to bring His people into heaven but to bring heaven to the earth.

Rather, God doesn't only want His people to be with Jesus, He also wants Jesus to be with His people (on earth), dwelling in humble and contrite hearts (Isaiah 57:15). Again, God is not simply interested in bringing His people to heaven, but He is also working to bring the government of heaven to the earth. "For unto us a Child is born, Unto us a Son is given; And the government will be upon His shoulder" (Isaiah 9:6). "On earth as it is in heaven" (Matthew 6:10).

Glory

God also wants to share the glory of Christ with the people of Christ. But why? It should be noted that the glory given to Christians is not their own glory, but the glory of Christ. We shall behold the glory of Christ because His glory is the capstone of salvation. In the completion of God's plan of salvation through Christ, God's glory will be complete. God will get all the glory because He will have completed His original plan. He will have made the final touchdown and won the game. All glory will go to the Redeemer who will unite heaven and earth in spiritual unity.

In that day, the people of Christ will be made perfect. The righteousness borrowed from Christ will then have completely colored and transformed the character of Christ's people. Baptized in the blood of Christ, the sins of the faithful will be as white as snow. The end of Christianity—fellowship with God through Christ—is the means of

Christianity—fellowship with God through Christ. It begins and ends with knowing Jesus Christ as personal Lord and Savior.

It begins in unity with Christ. Each individual believer must be in unity with Christ. That's Christian unity. If it doesn't begin there, it doesn't begin at all. But once it begins there Christian unity moves in ever increasing concentric circles of influence. It doesn't suddenly jump to national or denominational unity. Rather, it moves next to unity with your spouse. Then to unity with your children and parents. Then to unity with your friends and neighbors. Here is the unplowed ground of Christian unity and the fallow ground of Christian evangelism!

Proximity

Have you ever noticed that it is easier to be in unity with someone far away than it is to be in unity with your own household? Jesus calls His people to the more difficult task, Christian unity at home. Can you imagine the difference it would make if we could experience Christian unity in our families?! That's our goal. For a season forget denominational unity, forget unified missions in South America, or wherever. Forget political unity among the churches. And for a season, concentrate on unity with your husband or wife, unity with your sons and daughters, your parents and grandparents.

This is where Christian unity and evangelism are lost in our day—on the home front. The greatest loss of membership, the primary reason for the decline of Christian churches is that our own children have not come to know Christ. We have lost our own children. But it's not just us, it's been this way for generations! And it continues right under our own noses.

We know the difficulty of the homefront battle, and if we have chosen to fight at all, most have chosen an easier front, a more distant front. But Christ calls His people to Christian unity, first in personal relationship with Him, and then in the families of the faithful. Rather than bypassing this most difficult front, it is time that we reclaim our homes for Christ, reclaim our families for Christ. "He who has ears to hear, let him hear!" (Matthew 13:9).

The day is drawing nigh, and the final exam at the judgment seat of Christ will not consist of theological argumentation. It will not be a final test of theology—although theology is extremely important. Rather, at the judgment seat Christ will call your husband or your wife, your sons and your daughters, your parents and your grandparents, your friends and your neighbors to testify to your integrity and faithfulness.

What will they say?

August 25, 1996

Books by Phillip A. Ross

It's About Time! — The Time Is Now

40 pages. 2008.

This book is about thinking about God, the gospel, and Jesus Christ. We all need to make more time to do that. It is for the Mid-Ohio River Valley, but it is also for every valley where people live. It comes to a valley perspective from a valley perspective. This booklet is not about a mountaintop experience nor is it from a mountaintop perspective. Rather, it is from the "street," down in the valley where people actually live. It is not sad or morose, but it is serious—and it's about sin, yours and mine. It is an invitation to think more deeply about the things that we deeply care about, the things we believe. It's about Jesus.

These essays were originally written in 1998 as a short sermon series during Advent. They are not the usual Advent presentation of well-worn platitudes and biblical pablum. Unlike too many of my peers, I can't stomach that kind of stuff. To me, warm milk not only tastes bad, but it makes me sleepy.

This booklet is about the time in which we live. Hopefully, you will find it to be timely in your own life, as well. Time is a funny thing. We all live in it. Most of us are slaves to it, driven by appointments and schedules that must be kept. Asking people to think about time is like asking a fish to think about water—with one important difference. As far as we know, fish can't think at all, at least not in the way that we define thinking. I will ask you to think about time, about how much time you have, how much you need, and what you do with it.

Engagement—Establishing Relationship in Christ

104 pages, 1996, 2008.

The material in this book is not my usual fare, but was an attempt to put my best understanding of Scripture and salvation in Christ into a succinct format for a church that did not know me. It is not a expositional book study, but is more of a topical study intended to speak to the needs of contemporary people by uncovering various biblical truths and at the same time revealing various contemporary misunderstandings about the Bible and salvation.

As you will come to understand, it created quite a stir among those who heard it. But it did not generate church renewal or revival, at least not in the way that anyone would notice, not in what are considered to be the measures of renewal and revival. Rather, many hearers found it quite disturbing, and I then found myself in defensive mode as it seems to have raised more questions that it answered.

What you will see here is a synopsis of the historic, Protestant, Reformed position. If it seems unusual it is more likely because this theological position has been all but abandoned by the vast majority of contemporary Christians and their churches over the past 20, 50 or 100 years, depending on where you live and what circles you fellowship in.

The Big Ten—A Study of the Ten Commandments

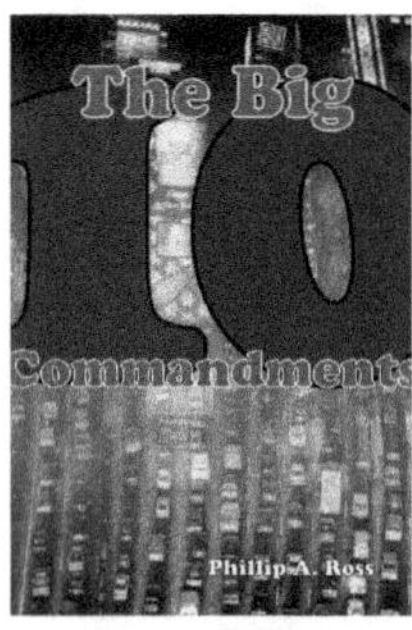

105 pages, 2001, 2008.

We live in an age of increasing lawlessness. It is not simply that there is a void of law, far from it. Quite the opposite is actually true. There is an overwhelming preponderance of laws, the size, scope and complexity of which world has never before seen. The body of law for any modern country, and in particular the United States—the most litigious society in history—is phenomenal. So, how can I say that we live in an age of increasing lawlessness?

What is in view here is not human law, but God's law. Just to speak the phrase brings a chill upon many a backbone. People don't like to talk about God's law. To do so is to be branded a fundamentalist, legalist, theonomist and/or extremist, all in the most vile sense of the words. For the most part contemporary Christians believe that they have arrived at a time in history that is beyond the application of any Old Testament laws, and in many cases, a time that is beyond all biblical law. People have converted the gospel of grace to mean a gospel without law—without obligation or responsibility.

The good news that is preached in too many pulpits today is lawlessness, couched in terms of a gospel of positive thinking, of upbeat moralisms intended to make life better, richer, fuller, more meaningful, and happier. In order to justify the human distaste for biblical law, people—Christians among them—no longer speak of God's law or the human obligation to it, not even in Bible study or worship.

However, the Bible is not a divided witness. It is a whole, a unity. God's Word, God's testimony is completely true.

The Wisdom of Jesus Christ in the Book of Proverbs

414 pages, 2006.

This study of Proverbs is an attempt to uncover the biblical message of Proverbs verse by verse in the light of Jesus Christ. We cannot pretend to be other than Christians who live on the redemption side of the Cross, while Proverbs was written on the anticipation side of the Cross. Nonetheless, the Christian faith is founded on the eternal consistency of God. God does not change. The God of Solomon, the author (and editor) of Proverbs, is the same God spoken of in the New Testament. In fact, the God of Solomon is Jesus Christ by the power of the Holy Spirit. Thus, the present work acknowledges this fact of faith and applies it by reading Proverbs in the light of Jesus Christ.

Marking God's Word—Understanding Jesus

324 pages, 2006.

Contemporary Western churches are a wreck, regardless of denominational affiliation or lack thereof. Mainline churches have been in serious decline for 50 years. The so-called contemporary churches are simply picking up transfer growth from other churches. Saying that there is a problem is one thing, but clearly defining the problem is something else. That something else is the subject of Marking God's Word. Clearly, there is much confusion in and out of the church about Christianity. Is confusion about the gospel of Jesus Christ new to the Modern and/or Postmodern world? That is the question that has haunted this treatment of Mark. *Marking God's Word* will help you see the gospel with new eyes, from a perspective that is obscured by sin and selfishness. Yet, this is not a new perspective. Rather, it is an old perspective that has a long and noble history of reformation and revival. Come, see Christ again, for the first time.

Acts of Faith—Kingdom Advancement

326 pages, 2007.

Acts of the Apostles continues the story of Jesus after His death. The story of the misunderstanding of the gospel among those who personally knew Jesus continues in the ministry of Paul. Paul, who was knocked off his high horse and thrown to the ground against his will and born again by the power of the Holy Spirit, came to see that he had been completely blind, and had his eyes miraculously opened. Paul – formerly the chief enemy of Christ, who became the chief disciple—took up the ministry and perspective of Jesus and began preaching the message of Christ to anyone who would listen. But Paul had the same difficulties that Jesus had—people thought he was crazy, that he didn't know what he was talking about, that he had gotten the gospel mes-sage wrong. Paul was hounded to death by the enemies of Christ, just as Jesus had been. Again, what is discovered in Acts of Faith is not a new perspective on Paul, but a very old one—the forgotten perspective of God's remnant.

Informal Christianity—Refining Christ's Church

136 pages, 2007.

Informal Christianity reviews the personal and informal realities involved in a personal relationship with Jesus Christ that provide the foundation of Christianity. Where the internal and subjective realities of regeneration are absent from the lives of church members, churches find themselves on a foundation of sand. Such churches turn away from the heart of Christianity — doctrine and theology — to focus on peripheral concerns of administration and maintenance. Christians and churches that do not enthusiastically embrace biblical doctrine and theology as the life-blood of faithfulness, tend to spend their time and energy polishing the outside of the cup (Matthew 23:25). Such efforts concern themselves with church growth — noses and nickels — rather than Christian maturity (Ephesians 4:13).

Informal Christianity aims to drive a nail through the heart of such trivial indulgence on the part of those who fail to live up to the potential of their Christian calling because such a failure amounts to the denial of the power and presence of the Holy Spirit in their own lives. Yes, the flesh is weak, no one is disputing that. But "the spirit indeed is willing" (Matthew 26:41). Christians "receive power when the Holy Spirit has come upon" (Act 1:8) them. Such power is the "strength that God supplies" (1 Peter 4:11). To wallow in administrative trivialities is to deny the power of God (Mark 12:24) and to deny one's citizenship in the Kingdom of God.

While great effort is being poured into the administrative expansion of churches (church growth), the very heart of personal faithfulness is being ignored, denied, denigrated and trivialized by the very principles that have been adopted to generate such growth. The proper priorities and first things (Matthew 6:33) are giving way to the "wisdom of men" (1 Corinthians 2:5). Informal Christianity cuts through the trees that have become veritable logs in the eyes of contemporary Christians to reveal again the forest of faithfulness in which the life of Christianity dwells.

Practically Christian—Applying James Today

135 pages, 2006.

Practically Christian offers a fresh and insightful application of the ancient Christian epistle of James to the contemporary American Evangelical world. Against the Antinomian backdrop of a Christianity shaped by the Church Growth Movement, Practically Christian puts teeth into Christianity, pressing for a practical realism in order to re-store some theological balance and sanity to the practice of the faith.

"Practically Christian offers a fresh and insightful application of the ancient Christian epistle to the contemporary American evangelical world. Against the Antinomian backdrop of a Christianity shaped by the church growth movement, Ross puts teeth into Christianity, pressing for a practical realism in order to restore some theological balance and sanity. His book is by no means dull reading or trite, but is replete with fresh anecdotes illustrating the salient points he is conveying. I found his exposition of James 1:2-4 to be especially instructive and profound, and on that basis alone the book was worth reading. Ross's commitment to Reformed doctrine is quite obvious throughout. Many parts of the book I wish I had written myself!" —David C. Brand, Pastor and author

Arsy Varsy—Reclaiming The Gospel in First Corinthians

399 pages, 2008.

"Corinth was a city of wealth and culture, seated at the crossroads of the Roman Empire, where all the trade and commerce of the empire passed through. It was a city of beauty, a resort city, located in a very beautiful area, but it was also a city of prostitution and of passion. It was devoted to trade and commerce, but also to the worship of the goddess of sex" (*The Corinthian Crisis*, by Ray Steadman).

Paul had a problem with the Christians at Corinth. They were a large, successful church. They were growing leaps and bounds. They thought they were doing great. But not Paul. Paul found that they had substituted the wisdom of the world (the philosophy and culture of the Greeks) for the wisdom of Christ (the philosophy and culture of the Bible). This volume contrasts the folly of Greek (and ultimately modern American) worldly wisdom with the gospel of Christ. Stones are turned over and small-minded creatures that thrive in the dark scatter in the light of Christ.

Ross brings Paul's struggle to light with clarity and passion that leaves the worldly no where to hide in this panoptic treatment to First Corinthians.

Varsy Arsy—Proclaiming The Gospel in Second Corinthians

356 pages, 2009.

Paul continued the same thrust of his criticism and correction in his Second Letter to the Corinthians, apparently because the same problems continued to dog the church. Paul's Second Letter is more personal as he ramped up the tone and clarity of his criticism. At one point he thought that he may have overstepped the bounds of propriety and apologized for his curtness—but not for his correction. Personal attacks against Paul, against him personally and the style and content of his ministry, had continued. So, Paul addressed them with clarity and severity.

The Jews and the Greeks provided substantial difficulties for Paul's ministry. But worse than those who had blatantly refused to conform to the light of Christ were those who disguised themselves as apostles of Christ, those who thought that they were helping the cause of Christianity by redefining it to fit into their own ill-conceived ideas. Apparently, the errant Corinthian leaders had been involved in these kinds of creative adaptations of the gospel. As much as Jesus had opposed the Pharisees, Paul opposed the false apostles. Both were guilty of perverting the doctrines and wisdom of Scripture.

Before we think that this idea is impossible because it is so outrageous, we need to realize that this *modus operandi* is not at all unusual. Satan's methodology has always been to counterfeit the truth because he has no truth or light himself. Satan goes the extra mile to make his wisdom look like Christ's wisdom—and many people are fooled by it (Matthew 24:24, 2 John 1:7), "as the serpent deceived Eve by his cunning" (2 Corinthians 11:3). It's the same old same old, a different instance of the same thing.

Against this backdrop, Paul clarified and reclaimed the true gospel, bringing to light many of the common errors that continue to haunt the church in our own day.

The Work At Zion—A Reckoning

Two-volume set, 772 pages, 1996.

The Work at Zion is the journal of a spiritual conversion that turned a ministry upside down. This collection of sermons details a preacher's rediscovery of classic, historical, Protestant Christianity in the midst of apathy and apostasy. The logical conclusion of modern Christianity is brought to a head and set in stark contrast to God's Word.

Sin is always the key to receiving Jesus. When people do not believe themselves to be sinners, they perceive no need for Jesus. The modern secular world has done everything it can to eradicate sin from modern awareness. Secular psychologists and educators insist that sin is outdated, that the doctrine of the Fall overly emphasizes the negative, to the detriment of personal self-esteem. But this modern, secular theory runs directly counter to the teaching and testimony of scripture. Scripture shows us that the confession of personal sinfulness is a prerequisite for salvation in Christ.

www.ingramcontent.com/pod-product-compliance
Lightning Source LLC
LaVergne TN
LVHW020645100826
845148LV00012B/2342

* 9 7 8 0 9 8 2 0 3 8 5 2 9 *